D1053293

JEWISH ENCOUNTERS

Jonathan Rosen, General Editor

Jewish Encounters is a collaboration between Schocken and Nextbook, a project devoted to the promotion of Jewish literature, culture, and ideas.

JEWISH ENCOUNTERS

The Wicked Son

DAVID MAMET

THE WICKED SON

Anti-Semitism, Self-Hatred,
and the Jews

NEXTBOOK · SCHOCKEN · NEW YORK

Copyright © 2006 by David Mamet
All rights reserved. Published in the United States by
Schocken Books, a division of Random House, Inc., New York,
and in Canada by Random House of Canada Limited, Toronto.

Schocken Books and colophon are registered trademarks of
Random House, Inc.

Library of Congress Cataloging-in-Publication Data
Mamet, David.
  The wicked son : anti-Semitism, self-hatred, and the
  Jews / David Mamet.
        p.   cm.—(Jewish encounters)
  ISBN 0-8052-4207-4
  I. Jews—Identity.   2. Self-hate (Psychology).
3. Antisemitism.   I. Title.   II. Series.
                DS143.M225 2006
                305.892'4—dc22

                                    2006043307

                www.schocken.com
        Printed in the United States of America
                    First Edition
            2   4   6   8   9   7   5   3

THIS BOOK IS DEDICATED TO
Meirav and Mordechai Finley

וכלם מקבלים עליהם
על מלכות שמים זה מזה . . .

CONTENTS

Contents

The Four Sons of the Haggadah

The rebbe was plagued by mice. The mice were eating his books, and nothing could dissuade them.

He searched in vain for a deterrent.

Until, reading the Shulkhan Arukh, he came across the statutes governing Passover.

The Shulkhan Arukh unequivocally states that nothing may be eaten after the afikomen.

So the rebbe crumpled the afikomen and sprinkled the crumbs over his books.

But the mice were smarter than the rebbe; first they ate the Shulkhan Arukh, then they ate the afikomen, and then they ate his books.

—As told by RABBI LAWRENCE KUSHNER

In the section of the Passover Haggadah called "The Four Sons," we find "What are the laws, the ordinances and the rulings which Hashem has commanded us?"

The answer being, "You should inform this child of all the

laws of Pesach, including the ruling that nothing should be eaten after the *afikomen*."

Passover Haggadah, the Feast of Freedom, the Rabbinical Assembly.

The wise child asks for information, and, in my Haggadah, he receives information, humor, which is to say, welcome to his tradition. His desire to learn and participate is rewarded with love—the other sons present their requests as if information were going to cure them of their anomie. Estrangement, hurt, rancor, alienation from the world, can, in the other-than-wise, be misinterpreted as, and assigned to, a failure of their tradition.

The second of the four sons, the wicked child, asks "What does this ritual mean to *you*?"

He is wicked in that his question is rhetorical—it is not even a request for information; it is an assault.

The wicked Jewish child removes himself from his tradition, and sets up as a rationalist and judge of those who would study, learn, and belong. Here is a joke for him.

The Minsker apikoros met the Pinsker apikoros. "I challenge your claim to preeminence," said the Minsker; "defend your excellence as an apikoros.

"I'm not sure I believe in God," said the Pinkser.

"*I'm* not sure *I* believe in God," replied the Minsker. "*And* I eat pork, I work on Shabbos, and I never go to shul."

"You aren't an apikoros," said the Pinkser. "You're a goy."

The third son is the simple son, who asks simply, "Ma Hu?" or "What *is* this?"

We are told to tell him, "It is with a mighty hand that Hashem took us out of Egypt, out of the house of bondage."

A borscht belt joke: Why did the Jews wander forty years in the desert? Because they wouldn't ask directions.

This is good, accurate ethnic humor; but it is not true that the Jews wandered forty years. They spent five weeks journeying between the Sea of Reeds and the Jordan River. Where Moses sent out the scouts. The scouts returned and said that the giants inhabited the land, that the scouts looked to themselves as grasshoppers and that they felt that so they must seem in the eyes of the giants.

Rabbi Finley teaches that this sin, of lack of faith, this inability to change, kept the Israelites in the desert, until God saw that the generation of the desert had died off, that time had killed the sin of acceptance of Slavery.

A new generation had been born that had never seen Egypt, and these people were educable and simple enough to ask, "What is this?"

The fourth child is he who does not know how to ask. For him, one is supposed to open the discussion.

To the wicked son, who asks, "What does all this mean to *you*?" To the Jews who, in the sixties, envied the Black Power Movement; who, in the nineties, envied the Palestinians; who weep at *Exodus* but jeer at the Israel Defense Forces; who nod when Tevye praises tradition but fidget through the seder; who might take their curiosity to a dogfight, to a bordello or an opium den but find ludicrous the notion of a visit to the synagogue; whose favorite Jew is Anne Frank and whose second-favorite does not exist; who are humble in their desire to learn about Kwanzaa and proud of their ignorance of Tu Bi'Shvat; who dread endogamy more than incest; who bow the head reverently at a baptism and have never attended a bris—to you, who find your religion and race repulsive, your ignorance of your history a satisfaction, here is a book from your brother.

The Wicked Son

In or Out?

The Jewish religion was admirably suited for defence, but it was never designed for conquest; and it seems probable that the number of proselytes was never much superior to that of apostates.

Yet even in their alien state, the Jews, still asserting their lofty and exclusive privileges, shunned, instead of courting, the society of strangers. They still insisted, with inflexible rigor, on those parts of the law which it was in their power to practice. Their peculiar distinction of days, of meats, and of a variety of trivial though burdensome observances, were so many objects of disgust and aversion for the other nations, to whose habits and prejudices they were diametrically opposite . . . under these circumstances, Christianity offered itself to the world, armed with the strength of Mosaic law, and delivered from the weight of its fetters.

—EDWARD GIBBON,
The Decline and Fall of the Roman Empire, Chapter 15

A s you have taken the time to read and I to write this book, I believe we should be frank: The world hates the Jews. The world has always and will continue to do so.

"Why?" is the question of the nonaffiliated, for to ask the question, is, in effect, to suggest there is an answer worthy of consideration. One does not ask of the school bomber, "What does he have against small children?"; of Hirohito, "What did he have against Pearl Harbor?" Neither did the victims of apartheid or Jim Crow attempt to understand their persecutors. Neither does the contemporary gay or lesbian attempt to understand the unreasoning hatred that he or she suffers and that expresses itself as right reason.

The effort to combat psychotic prejudice with reasonable counterarguments is not only an act of folly but a capitulation. (cf. The old saw "A woman who consents to listen consents.") We might say the world hates the unknown, the hermetic, the odd; we might say that Christianity and Islam, deriving from the mother religion, must indict that heritage too strict a toleration of which would gainsay their foundation doctrines; we might say that it is convenient to have an always-indictable Other upon whom one may project uncomfortable impulses, to have a race conveniently identified as savage, whose property, thus, may be appropriated at leisure—the Jew as "Mama's Bank Account." In this novella, filmed as *I Remember Mama*, Mama stills her family's fear of poverty by reference to their safety net—Mama's bank account—which is revealed at the story's end to be nonexistent. But, finally, there are but two options: to avow or to discount the notion that the world hates the Jews. The observant must, we know, endorse the first.

There now are two dependent options: that this hatred is reasonable or unreasonable.

To elect the first, even with satisfying fiats or limits, is race prejudice. Would you say, reader, of African-Americans, Native Americans, Mexicans, or of *any race*, "We must, of course, in good conscience, admit, entre nous, that there are aspects of their race and rite that are unfortunate?" Of course not, and you may not, then, in consistency, if not in conscience, say it of the Jews. This leaves the second option—that this hatred is unreasonable.

In accepting this unfortunate but accurate assessment, one may indict and/or attempt to change the world. But one cannot reason a lunatic, or a congeries of the same, out of their delusion, for the delusion is the absence of reason. One may, then, accept that this persecution is inevitable and con-stant (now waxing, now waning, but inevitable) and decide how one will deal with it. One may side with oppressors or side with the oppressed.

"Yes, but, yes, but, yes, but," you may exclaim and attempt to revert to a previously discounted proposition, that there is something unhealthy, unnice—choose your term—meaning "provocative," about the Jews. That, in sum, we "bring it on ourselves." By which reversion you are safely reassumed into blind folly, and thus, self-exempted from the work of either perception or action.

The attraction of flight, as Jonah from Ninevah, as Abraham from the imminence of God's pronouncements, is the burden of the Jews. It is not that we, uniquely, have been given the burden but that we, uniquely, have been *ordered to resist*.

Yes, the world hates you.

It may intermittently award the Jew the mantle of pseudo human being, (cf. Albert Einstein, and the State of Israel, 1948–1953), but the observant will find the very exercise of this dubious prerogative an example of race superiority.

The world hates the Jews.

You have been taxed, as the African-American was not, with the ability to "pass"; or better, with the illusion that you can do so. To avail yourself of the same is to be in a position similar to a homosexual in the church or in the army: the majority culture has "allowed" you a provisional membership, provided that you *never* pursue your proclivities. (Note also that, like the homosexual under "don't ask, don't tell," your very nature has been indicted as loathsome, and that which presents itself as an indulgence is, thus, a vicious expression of loathing.)

The world hates the Jews. The everyday announcements of the so-called "cycle of violence" in Israel are race slander, a pro forma reminder of the availability of the Jews as an object of disgust. They are, in this, like those Victorian novels, each of which featured a stock Jew—there hook-nosed and greasy, here intent on theft and murder. The indictments of Israel, in her life-and-death struggle, are unanswerable, as they are based upon a false assumption: that the uninvolved are somehow impartial.

"Can so many non-Jews be wrong?" you ask, and I would suggest that you consider the Shoah, the rape victim, the schoolchildren killed at Columbine. Is it reasonable to ask of the victims of Columbine, "What did they and their parents do to bring it about?"

Then you may not ask it of the Israeli bombing victims, and of their race and nation.

The world hates the Jews.

In or out.

The Other

> I was scandalized at the Sabbath in Sahariya . . . after three months in Jerusalem it was quite a sight; cafés open, singers in clubs, people in general amusing themselves . . . such a godless town! I guess it is that Jerusalem is a particularly Holy place . . . the peace and quiet that comes over Jerusalem at sundown on Friday night is like snow falling gently in Virginia.
>
> —MARY CLAWSON, *Letters from Jerusalem*

Mary Clawson's *Letters from Jerusalem* is a remarkable book. Clawson was a Christian woman, the wife of an agriculturist in the U.S. Foreign Service. He was posted to Jerusalem, and the book is a compilation of her letters home between 1952 and 1954.

She writes of her love for the Jew, of our national courage, humor, solidarity, invention, and hardiness. She comes to Israel and to the Jewish people curiously unprejudiced and finds us both admirable and human—two qualities today's

Western world is hardpressed to discover in the Jews, or in our lightning rod, the Jewish State.

Rabbi Kushner taught that the miracle of the burning bush was not that it was not consumed but that Moses watched it long enough to *perceive* that it was not consumed.

It must be true of all races, and I know it is true of mine, that its true excellences may not be immediately apparent to the prejudiced, indeed, to the merely uninvolved. Racial traits, observances, and philosophy may be understood as "bad," or merely obstinate. These quick, prejudiced opinions are destructive of justice; the enlightened have long recognized the error of ascribing a noxious trait or action of an individual to his race. Unfortunately, it requires further self-scrutiny to recognize that *any* observable and actual actions of race are easy to misunderstand, or mischaracterize, and that the human capacity for xenophobia is vast and we are usually eager to label the other as savage. (The designation "charming" is merely an application of the epithet of savagery to that group by which one does not currently feel threatened.)

The resourceful and quaint little Annamese became the Gooks, as Hans und Fritz of the Edwardian vaudeville became the hated Hun, as Tevye the Milkman became, once again, the bloodthirsty, insatiable "Jew," fiend of the Middle East.

The most enlightened of intellects are not protected from the virus of ethnocentrism, merely substituting "it is plain" for the "everybody knows" of the less educated. Contemporary fashionable sentiment in the West denigrates the

Jewish State and, thus, consciously or not, the Jew. This is but a regression to the mean, a world correction of the anomaly of twenty or thirty years of post-Shoah sympathy, after 2,000 years of persecution at the hands of the Christian West.

The historic endorsement of and, indeed, demand *for* persecution of those whose religion preceded the Gospels is now, perhaps unconsciously but nonetheless reified in the Christian West by fear of a jihadist Arabia. The Arab's anti-Semitism is an internecine feud, waxing and waning over millenia. The Arab military humiliation at the hands of Israel, cross-grafted with Christian doctrinal Jew-hatred has been treated magnificently by Islamic scholar Bernard Lewis (notably in his books *What Went Wrong* and *Semites and Anti-Semites.*)

These Christian and Moslem doctrinal prejudices and geopolitical grievances are joined and, unfortunately in the minds of some, ratified by what would otherwise (absent the global oil situation) be understood as a pitiable if vocal minority: apostate Jews whose denunciation of Israel rises past legitimate debate into the realm of race treason. Such are treasonous not in disagreement with contemporary Israeli policies (such disagreement is a salient fact of life in Israel, as abroad), but in the designation, by the apostate, of his coreligionists, his racial brothers, as the Other.

The apostate feels himself superior to that Other which is his race and clan, and glories in his profession of exile. Eric Hoffer wrote in the sixties of the tendency of the self-aggrandizing to turn on their own group, seeking notoriety and endorsement for their magnificent detachment. Such "fair-mindedness" contains a refusal to recognize, in their brothers and sisters, the anguish of their situation and the imperfection of their solutions as they engage in a literal battle for their lives.

This inability to assign to the Israelis a basic humanity is, to me, more deeply disturbing than the reluctance to endorse or accept any of their national positions. The happy assignment of wicked motives to the Israeli soldier, command, and populace is, to me, more deeply troubling than the fraudulent misreportage of actual acts as savage.

Do, can, or could the Israelis delight in "reprisals," in "retaliation"? The very words are revelatory, for such actions by the United States are known as "defense"—a country defends itself; reprisals and retaliation are the actions of a mob. And, if the actions of the Israelis are strategically, or indeed morally, imperfect, could their detractors, put in the same position, suggest or implement better?

The outright denunciation of Israel as "acquisitionist, bloodthirsty, colonial, et cetera" is to me simply a modern instance of the blood libel—that Jews delight in the blood of others. The world was told Jews used this blood in the performance of religious ceremonies. This libel gained currency in the West due, inter alia, to the efforts of Henry Ford and his campaign against the Jews; it has been newly adopted by much of the Arab world and is taught and broadcast (Moslem blood taking the place of Christian) in various

Middle Eastern propaganda and schools and, indeed, in much of the so-called liberal press.

As the outright currency of this canard waned in the West, its utility was preserved in the shift from a religious to a political attack. Now, it seems, Jews do not require the blood for baking purposes; they merely delight to spill it on the ground for some magical, nefarious, and diabolical reason. The treatment of the Jews as vampire has, on analysis, much of the "as you know . . ."; for, if one did not "know" that Jews are subhuman, why would one entertain this bizarre accusation?

Imagine the anti-Israeli propaganda currently engaged in on college campuses and other institutions of enlightenment—directed against Canada—not that Canadians are misguided, wrong, but that they are "bad"—devoid of the capacity for goodwill, duplicitous, inspired by some nefarious and implacable power to wrong those around them; possessed of a power so diabolical it induces their neighbors to strap bombs on their young and send them into the marketplace to slaughter women and their babies.

What is this power? It must be the Devil; indeed, it *is* the Devil, and the Jews will not stop until they have ruined the world.

It is not that the "Jew is bad" but that we human beings are imperfect, easily stampeded, and incapable of ascribing our unreasoning fear to anything other than reason. The conceit of the "bad Canadians" may seem ludicrous—how ever could the friendly Sergeant Preston of the Yukon, known of old, become a monster? But it needed only a few days of government diatribe to wipe out the traditional archetype of "our friend the jolly Frenchman" with his loaf of crusty bread and to send the newly aroused pouring Chablis down the drain. And have not the middle-aged gay couple next door, whose happy commitment we witnessed over twenty years, now become that monstrous threat to the "institution of marriage"?

The thus-afflicted individual—the victim of jingoism—is enraged not by the newly revealed threat *but by his loss of autonomy*. Torn between a desire for safety, which has been presented as the necessity to conform, and its price, which is abdication of reason, the individual becomes enraged and, voting for conformity, explains and expresses his rage against the newly proclaimed Other. It was a semantic masterstroke to label a law destructive of our Constitution the U.S.A. Patriot Act, for provisions that would be rightly seen as outrageous in an act designed to promote *security* were passed when to oppose them would have been to risk the appellation "traitor." The appellation of the act threatened the autonomy of the unconvinced legislators and permitted them to express their otherwise inexpressible rage against the Other (the terrorist).

The Jewish State has offered the Arab world peace since 1948; it has received war, and slaughter, and the rhetoric of annihilation. After fifty-six years of war this tiny fingernail of a country, the size of Vermont, continues to exist *and to practice democracy* in spite of the proclaimed implacable hatred of an Arab world rich, vast, and populous.

Enlightened university opinion in the West indicts Israel as an aggressor. This is a fantasy similar to that of the Insatiable Black. This black, sexual monster, who wished only to rape white women, was still an absolute article of white American faith at a time within my memory.

I recall seeing an African-American jazz combo in a nightclub in Chicago in the 1950s. The leader said they'd just returned from a tour of the South, and that when they played "I've Got My Eye on You," they better have been looking at each other.

American white men, slaveholders, and others had of course raped African-American women over centuries as a droit du seigneur. And the ascription to the black man of an insatiable, demonic sexuality was among other things an attempt at self-license. It also posited a universe the operative mechanic factor of which was ungovernable lust, so that, in terrorizing the black, the white was enlisting the "inevitable" in the cause of Good, was teaching, in effect, a religious lesson.

Similarly, Christian and Moslem fulfill a religious duty in scourging the supposed sin of the Jew, that sin not lust but avarice. For this is the unstated epithet: just as the American black man was a slave to sex, so is the Jew a slave to his lust for property, and his monstrous, constant crimes against the Palestinians proof positive of his taint—inexplicable other than as a malignant genetic mutation.

The "crimes" of Israel, as those of the African-American man, are imaginary, existing in the mind of the accuser and engendered both by his guilt at his oppressive behavior and by his attempt to license his own criminal passions.

The rhetoric of sad reason, that Israel is an "experiment that has failed," is but the coward end of a spectrum whose bold extension is "kill all the Jews and drive them into the sea." The first, in addition to being a racially derogatory epithet, is additionally a goad and a sop to the second. For Israel is not an "experiment"; it is a country. Ben-Gurion said, in the late forties, that the world was divided into two halves, those places the Jews could not stay and those to which they could not go. What has changed? The world still hates the Jews.

The change is the State of Israel, and, regarding it, the anti-Semite finds a protected voice. He may write anti-Jewish propaganda and, at will, publish and peruse it with a smug delight.

"Mr. Sharon (who had ignited the powderkeg of the intifada by entering the Haram-al-Sharif, Jerusalem's holiest Muslim site)," from *The Economist*, 28 March 2006. This organ of supposedly reasonable discourse continues in what might seem, if not a supportable, a rational statement, though it has been established that Sharon did not transgress any site holy to the Moslems and it is universally known that the intifada had been planned for months before the supposed *causus belli*.

The repeated assertion of Sharon's murderous "walk" is the modern-day equivalent of the charge of well poisoning and the murder of Christian babies. It is only the most current rendition of the idea that "the Jews killed Christ"—it is the blood libel, and its purveyors, in their absolute refusal to think rationally, bear some responsibility for the deaths in the cafes of Tel Aviv.

One so disposed might read *The Economist*'s supercilious pronouncements on the pesky Israelis with a secret sense of glee, as a Victorian perhaps perused a nineteenth-century African adventure novel's description of "the shiftless niggers."

The contemporary reader aghast at such racism may nonetheless understand as right reason his excoriation of the Israeli "rape of Jenin," of savage Israeli soldiers driving the poor oppressed to greater and greater prodigies of terror.

The pure-hearted liberal who would die rather than endorse the wife beater's exculpatory "She just wouldn't listen" delights to extend his imprimatur to the atrocities of the jihadists. This is anti-Semitism.

It is, unfortunately, human nature to think the Other inhuman.

Our comfortable society has rationalized the tropism

thusly: that Other *that has been subdued* may be granted the status of the *picturesque*. The mechanism is seen in the idea of the noble savage, and in the Bold Mussulman of the Hills in the Edwardian novels of the Great Game in the contemporary fetish for Native American culture and philosophy, and in the idea of "diversity." Those who have been subdued need no longer be feared, and we, the majority culture, are now free to appropriate those last, late-appearing aspects of their worth for our own use and delight.

The image of the Arab totters today in the American consciousness. On the one hand, we have "the terrorist"—the bombers of New York; on the other, a poor, beleaguered peasant, in extremity forced to throw rocks against Israeli tanks.★

The Jew, for a brief moment, was, to the West, the noble savage—for example, *The Goldbergs, Potash and Perlmutter, Weber and Fields, Gentlemen's Agreement, Fiddler on the Roof, The Diary of Anne Frank*, and *Exodus. Exodus* (1960) was the turning point, when the Jewish State, obviously intent on continued existence, began to forfeit its protected status as colorful victim—wherein the world saw Jews assert our absolute right to exist.

For the Other may avail itself of various prerequisites of the majority culture (and this is the tacit bargain) only by asserting his powerlessness. He might gain grudging sup-

---

★ See also Victorian literature of the northwest frontier and its persistence, curiously, in the latest novel by John Le Carré, *Absolute Friends*.

port for affirmative action but will endanger that support by plumping for school vouchers—by demanding equality rather than requesting reparations. And our picturesque Native Americans may be awarded the sin franchise of our gambling casinos but become "uppity" when demanding land guaranteed by ancestral treaties.

World Jews, then, with the rise of the Jewish State, have become uppity. As Israel and its citizens continue to assert an absolute right to existence, much of the Western world withdraws what it is unable to understand was but a patronizing and cost-free consideration of a colorful victim.

The transition of Jew from amusing hard-luck denizen of the bazaar (see any Holocaust film) to pagan thug might indicate to the fickle West an incipient ethnocentrism.

We Jews are neither. And the Western nexus of amused contempt and loathing is unitary. The shift from the first toward the second does demonstrate the dawning of reason; it denotes a change not in the *conduct* but in the *status* of the Other. Contemporary Western loathing of Israel might reveal to the inquiring mind an ancient never-eradicated prejudice.

"How dare they disturb my morning coffee," says the West. "Did I not find them charming for so long—and this is how the swine repay me?"

Hide in Plain Sight

The memory of absolute wrongs causes absolute trauma in a race, just as in the individual. Incalculably ancient race memory of dinosaurs persists to this day, transformed as an affection for the dragon. Memory of the most traumatic of cultural acts, child sacrifice, can be seen, hidden in plain sight, as ceremonies of transformation, redemption, and, in fact, of jollity.★ Like the Santa Claus myth, the

---

★ The Santa Claus myth is a straightforward account of child sacrifice. It must, however, be read in the mirror. Children can be good or bad. They put their stockings out, and, in the middle of the night, a man comes into their home with a bag. If the child has been bad, the man puts the child in a sack and takes him away. All that is left of him is his stocking, hung on the foot of the bed. If this interpretation seems far fetched, please consider the parents' anxiety about the myth's "falsity." Christian parents may agonize over "when shall we tell the children" (that Santa is not real) and may, year by year, conclude, "There's time for that when they're older. Let them enjoy their innocence (their ignorance) a little longer." It is no great reach to see, here, the anguish of a family in antiquity, knowing the tribe will choose, at the winter solstice, some child to be sacrificed and to see the parents wish to extend the child's period of exemption from terror for as long as possible.

Akedah, the Crucifixion, are ineradicable race memories of infant sacrifice, and of the deeply buried wish to resume its practice, so racism must be the unresolved race memory of slavery.

The idea that one group of human beings could be the property of another must always have been a psychological burden, to the oppressors, to the oppressed and to those not overtly affected by it, save by their exposure to its corrosive presence in society. It is a testament to what can only be called "conscience" (understood as guilt) that the race memory of the affront persists, generations after the eradication of the actual practice.

Here is the internalized, persistent rationale of slavery: if a group has forfeited the most basic human rights, there must be something wrong with them.

This is a transformation from wonder (or pity) through reason to acceptance. It allows the confused to function with the burden of an otherwise unassimilable contradiction. It removes the necessity of either action or outrage; these, indeed, may be discharged not at the perpetrators but at the victims. Not, perhaps, because of any recognition of inherent evil on the victims' part but, to the contrary, because a recognition of their innocent humanity would force the onlooker to a knowledge of his own cowardice. And to the cowardice of the society whose benefits he enjoys.

Such a betrayal (by him, and of him by his society) cannot be forgotten. Like the trauma of infant sacrifice, it must be assimilated. The Western Christian world acts out this ceremony each year at the winter solstice, in its anxiety with the Santa Claus myth: "What shall we tell the children? Are they old enough to understand?"

Here we have an intergenerational, centuries-long ceremony of confusion of myth and reality. The myth, here, serves not to *integrate* the affronted consciousness but to *preserve* a trauma. It is the *contre-coup* to the outrage of child murder and its societal acceptance. The ancient, human desire to hide the truth from the children was so strong as to persist, thousands of years later, when the threat itself is gone. And the undischarged trauma of slavery (for all of the Western world, black or white) persists as racism; as the absolute certainty that if this or that group was so abused (cf. the Intifada) they must have brought it on themselves.

One may note that this is not *primarily* a reaction of the coward but of the *child*, who looks on at horror inflicted on another and at his parents' and his society's passive endorsement of the horror. To conclude that his parents and their society are depraved is beyond the child's imagining. They must, then, be correct. The true strength of race prejudice is that it is inculcated in childhood (before the possibility of rational judgment) and is inseparable from the child's need for security and for powerful and *moral* parents.

The adult, in persisting in inherited racism, upholds his parents, his society, and indicts that force (the victim) that would, by its very presence, convict them. African-Americans, in my lifetime, have been notably effective in the battle against race prejudice (in themselves and others) by, for example, the campaign "Black Is Beautiful." Their insistence on this phrase forced those who found it untrue or difficult to wonder at their strong reactions to a simple inoffensive formula.

The illness, racism, cannot be perceived by the sufferer. Racism and love make such perfect sense to those affected that the entire world is redefined in their light. The sufferer cannot perceive "their effect," for he *is* their effect. His consciousness, that mechanism whereby he might perceive them, is the afflicted organ.

Racism cannot be perceived. The sufferer, therefore, must reason backward from the behavior to the necessarily operative idea. This is too difficult. How can the busy, self-involved human being spend his day working toward a perception, the acceptance of which would entail self-revulsion and shame?

He will not. The laws of psychic economy ensure that his mind will, always, do the easier of two difficult things, and repress. This repression and its burdens are chronic rather than acute. It is transmitted from one generation to the next (cf. the Santa Claus myth).

The Akedah (the Torah story of the binding of Isaac) is an attempt to deal with the trauma of human savagery. Anti-Semitism is an attempt to deal with the Akedah. In the Akedah the Torah *lifts* the injunction against discussion of infant sacrifice and the hatred of the Western Christian world is turned, not against savagery but against *that force that would weaken the repressive power.*

That the Jews persist in the same religion which gave rise to Christianity and Islam is to their practitioners as little tolerable today as it was when these two schismatic professions split off from the mother faith. Jewish persistence is, thus, an indictment, to the affronted, prejudiced mind, of generations of his non-Jewish forebears who, were the Jews recognized as nonoffending, the adult child would now have to recognize as monstrous. For them, as for the Jew raised to hate his own, no "proof" will suffice. Remonstrations are often taken, indeed as further "proof" of Jewish subhumanity (here called "wiliness").

The wicked son ascribes his anomie to "the Jews," or, in a psychologically brilliant variation, to "Jewish guilt," that is, "to some nameless, terrible thing I, as a Jew, have inherited." Imagine this construction with some other group substituted for Jew. "My group, X, is so terribly, terribly bad, they have enjoined upon me some unnameable, wicked curse. They have cursed my soul."

If we substitute another word for "Jew," this formulation is revealed, of course, as voodoo. How can the wicked son observe his thoughts, feelings, and actions and compare them to an agreed-upon neutral norm (in effect, the essence of psychoanalysis)? For, *only* through doing so might he come to recognize their bizarre, insane aspect.

What can save the self-loathing Jew from his apostasy?

Reason will no more reach him than any other addict. Perhaps shock may work its unfortunately effective way with him. Perhaps the shock that he is bequeathing to his children, that same abuse to which he, as an unthinking child, was subject.

Jewish Anxiety

Anxiety is a universal disease, and the Jewish apostrophization of anxiety is an attempt to assimilate—but to what?

Pagan, which is to say, ineradicably human, ceremonies survive all around us. The American political circus is an attempt to discover or create a human without blemish and offer such as an opponent to the gods.

Religion has striven and strives to supplant human idolatry, which *constantly* reasserts itself; politics, similarly, is, now and again, the doomed and failing struggle to supplant paganism with reason.

Theoretically, political parties employ a candidate to promote a political platform, and the opposing candidates are judged both on that platform and on their ability to express it. Currently (and, we must suppose, intermittently throughout history), what was political discourse has devolved into each party and candidate calling attention to the other's lack of perfection. Drug use, sexual peccadilloes, youthful misdemeanors, or, indeed, inconsistencies are alleged against one's opponent. The candidate against whom such are proved or stand irrefuted is thus adjudged unfit to stand against the gods.

We note that the contemporary American electorate is uninterested in a candidate sufficiently intelligent to confront complexity. This lack of interest in a candidate's mental capacity might prove baffling, but let us reflect that no intelligence is required to act as a symbol. Intelligence in a symbol is irrelevant. Consider, for instance, Miss America, the First Lady, game show presenters—though their intelligence is beside the point, their purity must be unquestioned: Marilyn Chambers was the face on the Ivory Snow soapbox; her face was removed when it was discovered she had acted in pornographic movies.

The Right cast the late presidential contests as one concerning "values" and "morals." Such morals and values were inchoate, largely unspecified, and, when clear, identifiable as universal.

Why, then, should the Right predominate over the Left in the minds of "moral" voters? Not because their candidate possessed "more" of these values but because he was more willing to so cast the debate. For that debate was not an invitation to the electorate to judge the candidates against a stated standard but a call to the voter to observe which side was the more willing to so characterize the conflict.

Observe which side, the Right said, is the more willing to cast aside not only the historically irrelevant possession of reason but the *ethical elements of religion*—compassion, humility, forbearance—and to revert to a Manichaean fundamentalist understanding of the world.

This reversion is claimed, by the Right, as a return to a literal understanding of the Bible; in truth, however, it is a call to that paganism the Abrahamic religions superseded. "It's about morals," whether uttered by jihadists or the Christian Right, is a call to lay down the intolerable yoke of religion ("What is hateful to you, do not do to your neighbor") and to serve, once again, the One True God, the unquestioned self, its fears, and its appetites.

The least bearable burden of reason is the knowledge of one's own powerlessness: human intelligence, it may be seen, does not eradicate strife; where, then, does power lie?

Ultranationalism and fundamentalism are both attempts to find those hidden essentials of humanity whose abandonment has brought about this loathsome state we call the present. And the land, as of old, must be cleansed by blood.

The Crucifixion, like the Akedah, is an attempt to master the racial horror of infant sacrifice (the cleansing of the land by blood). If sacrifice is renounced (in the Christ story: "Don't you see what you have done?"; in the story of Isaac: "You may stop now"), the worshipper is left with a burden. The burden of this renunciation is not, primarily, shame ("Oh, my God, what was I considering?") but *longing*.

Obviously, and observably, the gods are angered as we, misguided, have neglected to feed them. Nor does our crime stop there: we have also listened to the rantings of those who have been embraced and counsel as a policy the replacement of sacrifice by "reason" (liberals, nonbelievers, Westerners, reformers in general).

There is an aesthetic quality in fundamentalism, in jingoism, in jihad—a pure joy in the rejection not only of reasoned religion but also, indeed, of science.

"Belief" is such a potent force that it may replace logic: we may burn the heretic books that speak of "evolution," and we may say the cost is huge: the loss of the scientific method, but this is not a loss at all but a *gain*, the repeal of the taxing concept of cause and effect. For Galileo may "prove" that the earth revolves around the sun, but we know, instinctively, the opposite is true; and religion may suggest we remove the mote from our own eye, but we *know* that the cause of strife is the Other.

The recrudescence of the pagan is seen with the approach of the winter solstice, where in the West, anxiety has regressed the Christ story into the Santa Claus myth.★

Assimilated or assimilationist Jews, another stratum of society, are anxious over "conflicting claims" of the two solstice holidays, Chanukah and Christmas: What shall we do? Are we needlessly depriving our children of a deserved "treat" by not celebrating Christmas? Are we being untrue to our heritage by considering celebrating it, should we not

---

★ This recrudescence may be seen in its virulence at the recurring inability of conflicted Jews to create, participate in, or sit through the Spring ceremony: the Passover seder.

give our children what must, rationally, be seen as the benefit of celebrating both holidays?

In falling victim to this anxiety the Jews are reverting, not to Christianity but to a universal horror at the waning of the sun—such anxiety vulgarized, in the Christian tradition, by the jolly story of Kris Kringle. (The 2005 Christmas movie *The Polar Express*, from the book by Chris Van Allsburg, is an eruption of the psychological underpinnings of the Santa myth. Here the children, who do not quite "believe," are taken away from their homes and, in effect, reeducated.)

It is not, finally, a yearning to "be like the Christians" that drives these conflicted winter Jews; they have simply fallen under the influence of the old gods. They strive, in their fog, *not* to come to a final decision about the presence or absence of the mistletoe, but to confess the sin of apostasy and to prostrate themselves, weeping, before the waning sun.

"Jewish guilt" and "Jewish anxiety" are not Jewish at all but universal—a universal desire to revert to paganism. It is not the Christians the Jews try to ape with their Chanukah bush but the pagans. The cure for the Jew is neither assimilation nor conversion, but *religion*.

Religion came into being to supplant the anomie and excess of paganism. Humans individually, and all religions they create, are always in a dynamic struggle between the desire to revert to, and the desire to supersede, the pagan.

The answer, for the Christian, is Christianity; for the Jew, Judaism.

Each may desire to revert. This yearning may lead the Christian to identify the cause of anxiety as the presence of heterodoxy, humanism, liberal humanism, or other descriptions of a church grown insufficiently rigorous; this Christian may seek solace in fundamentalism, as may the Jew. The Jew, however, is, in the main, less aware of his own religion and its opportunities for the fundamental. He is more likely to suppose that the "error" he finds in his religion can be cured only by his embrace of another.

The assimilated Jew, ignorant of his own religion, supposes solace in what he misunderstands as a universalist Christianity and labels his anxiety as error, and that error as "Jewish."

A Hot Hen's Kiss

There is a system of beliefs correlative to anti-Semitism, the contemplation of which may reveal the nature of both as mania. I refer to that of the Baconians or anti-Stratfordians. These believe that Shakespeare's plays were written by someone other than Shakespeare, the most vocal adherents of the faith plumping for Francis Bacon as the author.

This delusion dates back to at least the eighteenth century. And, as with other prejudice, it begins with a belief and proceeds to the manufacture of proofs. Anti-Stratfordians hold that it is impossible for Shakespeare to have written his plays because he had little formal education, he had little exposure to Court, he was not widely traveled, in short, that he was "not the right type."

Proceeding from conclusion to investigation, they cite or concoct various proofs of their theory. Notable among them is the Bacon Cipher.*

* I am indebted to William F. Friedman and Elizabeth S. Friedman, *The Shakespearean Ciphers Examined* (Cambridge University Press, 1957).

Francis Bacon, in *The Advancement of Learning*, sets forth a simple binomial cipher, composed of A's and B's. Plaintext A is *aaaaa*, B is *aaaab*, et cetera.

Now, consider the phrase, "How fine is the day."

Were we to capitalize some letters seemingly at random, we might find: "howfIne is the day." Now, if the lowercase letters signified A and the capitalized B, and we chopped up the message into groups of five letters, we would find: howfI neist heday—or—if lowercase equals A, and uppercase B, AAAAB AAAAA AAAAA, we now refer to our binomial cheat sheet where the alphabet is rendered in cipher. We find AAAAB = B, AAAAA = A, AAAAA = A, or "BAA," the cunning cryptographer having hidden the secret message, the sound of a sheep, "Baa," in a seemingly innocuous comment about the weather.

So far so good.

Unfortunately, however, various editions of Shakespeare were printed with little regard for capitalizations, and many in more than one font; and Baconians have found, in this accidental alternativeness, a binomial A-B cipher.

Applying this A-B binomial cipher to a page of plaintext Shakespeare, they discover this group of hidden letters: SASSOHHKINTE. The letters discovered, however, yield no meaning in this raw form. But perhaps they may be considered as an anagram, and rearranged to yield their sense.

The Baconians might anagram this apparent nonsense (SASSOHHKINTE) to yield the plaintext SHAKS IS

NOT HE; thus, by but a minor stretch, proving the anti-Stratfordian case.

The same letters, however, might, equally, be anagrammed A HOT HEN'S KISS. Proving not much of anything at all.

So, again, the Baconians start with a premise, peruse a text that they declare contains a cipher, find enciphered letters, and arrange them at random to establish the principle that was the initial inspiration for their efforts.

The Baconian A-B cipher is but one of a host of devices whereby the faithful find proofs for their theory of non-Shakespearean authorship. Others include a numeric system (like that suggested by various "Bible" codes, taking every Xth word, for example, and arranging them to suit), dreams, supernatural encounters, and so on.

But note the underlying enormity: (a) that a writer who, for the purposes of argument we will call "Shakespeare," the greatest writer the world has ever known, would craft his work as a pretext for the transmission of a secret message, and (b) that this message (let alone being moot) was, however extracted, *badly written.*

Why would a scholar indulge in such contortions, such inversion of the scientific method and of simple reason? Why engage in what is essentially a religious quest and call it the study of literature? For the same reason one engages in Jew-hatred, because of a *delusion of grandeur.* For what greater power (to the litterateur) than that to award the mantle of divinity?

This obsession can be seen in the various seminal irritations leading the scholar to the supposed proofs: that Shakespeare was insufficiently educated, insufficiently trained, and so on; which may be understood as "How *dare* this upstart . . ."

The possessed, then, proceeds to recognize in himself a heretofore unrecognized genius, that of detecting fraud among the wrongly celebrated, and raises himself to the post of Supreme Champion of Right. For what could be more laudable than to correct the most egregious error in the history of the world? Thus anti-Semitism, the Gospels, and Christian dogma (although somewhat mitigated by Vatican II), etc.

The Jew-hater begins with a proposition that glorifies and comforts him: that there exists a force of evil in the that that he has, to his credit, discovered and bravely proclaimed. In opposing it, he is self-glorified. This glory, like that of the Baconian's, is brought about by a simple profession (or, indeed, sentiment) of faith; one triumphs over evil, thus becoming as a god, at no cost other than recognition of his own divinity.

The actual proofs are secondary and may be indulged in ad libitum—they need not be either consistent or rational, and those demanding either in them may freely be reviled as nonbelievers, and, in the case of the Jews, persecuted, robbed, and killed.

What good to point out that "the Jews" could not have condemned Jesus on the Sabbath following Good Friday, as no court could be convened on the Sabbath; that no court could be convened during Passover; that deicide is an oxymoron; and on and on ad nauseam. The "proofs" exist merely to buttress a belief; the belief exists to license fantasy and the crime that it engenders.

Treason

> In the new Europe, the Jew probably will soon be a thing of the past. The remnants of this unhappy people will soon disappear. Many of them have been starved, many sterilized, and it is not to be supposed that they will keep their identity much longer. One wonders what group will be selected to act as the scapegoats when the Jews are all gone.
>
> —DOUGLAS MILLER,
> *You Can't Do Business with Hitler* (1941)

In Philip Roth's brilliant novel *Letting Go* (1962), the first-person protagonist, Gabe Wallach, is a wealthy, assimilated, Harvard-educated custom-tailored Jew. He is rather gormless, adrift in his view, in a glass-bottom boat in a swamp of Jewry. To him all Jews are risible, corrupt, sordid, misguided, or cruel.

Here the immigrant generation is, at all times, squabbling, self-obsessed, greedy, ill dressed, ill kempt. But the raisonneur, Gabe Wallach, the Jude Süss, the "light, bright and damn-near white," is the dispassionate observer from the Parnassus of Full Americanization. He lusts after Libby, the Jew-by-choice, the wife of his colleague Herz.

Libby's decision to convert is seen by Wallach, and by all the novel's other Jews, as a monumental error. She has gone to the mikvah in her Jantzen swimsuit. She marries Herz in a civil ceremony, as the rabbi to whom they have presented themselves for counseling excoriates Herz for apostasy and his betrothed for stupidity. Both sets of parents turn on them. Only Gabe, the dispassionate, assimilated Jew, sees through the squalor that their marriage has brought on them, his generosity of spirit inspired by a simple human urge: he wants to mount her.

He runs into her on Madison Street. She accompanies him shopping. He indulges himself, at Brooks Brothers, in a complete haberdashery, extending to smoking jacket, Homburg, and puce leather gloves. And Roth notes Libby's glee in his Anglophile self-indulgence, so far removed from that world of "oi-oi-oi" to which the little minx has, unwittingly, consigned herself.

The world of the immigrant generation is, to the novel's hero, a horror tale of close escapes and nonescapes from poverty, of intellectual and social gaffes and of communal misery. This vision is hurtful, unrelieved, and unsympathetic; it is an accurate portrayal both of the immigrant generation's trials and of their progeny's ingratitude.

The generation of my grandparents came from Europe

with nothing, and sent their sons not only to college, but thence into a conquest of the professions. This generation heroically survived and overcame the trials of immigration, of the Depression, of the War, armed with nothing but determination to succeed. They succeeded so far beyond their expectations that their sons became sufficiently Americanized as to loathe their parents.

Who is this Gabe Wallach, this modern man, so scornful of tradition, of filial respect, as to mock, not with loving irony but with vicious sarcasm, the ways of his forbears? And how virulent was and is this view?

For the idea of the risibility, first of the immigrant generation and then of its religion, was for its grandchildren the norm. The savaging of the Ashkenazi immigrants, in the novels of their children in the 1950s and '60s, bore fruit (inter alia) in the nebbish stage persona of various post–Borscht Belt comedians, a Jewish gloss on a generally accepted form of entertainment—racial indictment. Those old enough may recognize this type of impersonation, which used to be called, generically, "Amos and Andy." But the minstrel show, the "darky" turn in vaudeville, and *Amos and Andy* were the creations not of African-Americans but of whites.

Can one imagine African-Americans, the descendants of slaves, mocking their forebears' trials, and the fears and strategies both for accommodation and for self-respect, forged over two hundred years of inescapable bondage? Must not that trauma be respected?

How could one who had not experienced it treat the survivals of slavery with anything other than a profound, nonjudgmental respect? And might not the spared recognize, *in the culture that they had inherited*, phenomenal courage and invention rather (and more morally) than awkwardness and difference from the "majority culture"? For to today's African-American, though not to the Jew, the idea of "the majority culture" is, perhaps, recognizable as an illusion.

For what is the majority culture other than an accidental, moot, and, at best, transient confederation of the momentarily unchallenged? It is no culture at all but an assemblage of the fortunate under the illusion that they have something in common other than their luck.

True cultural identity, as familial identity, comes from absolute commitment. Assimilation that entails rejection of one's ancestors' sorrow, rather than a "ticket of admission" to the majority culture is an announcement of depravity.

Why does this emancipated Jew, Gabe Wallach, this or that comedian's stage clown—you or I, perhaps—turn his back on race and religion? What are his reasons? Watch, and he will confect intellectual, emotional, political, and aesthetic explanations.

The Jews in *Letting Go*, in the raisonneur's eyes, have neither manners nor understanding of the country they inhabit and affront. The State of Israel, Noam Chomsky informs the ignorant, is a crime; an independent "ex-Jew" explains that he "once met an unpleasant rabbi"; a theological freethinker asks how she can "believe in a god who would ask Abraham to murder his son?"

These are put forth as peremptory challenges, that is, each is considered sufficient *in its utterance* to exempt the speaker not only from filial piety but from the need of further investigation, explanation, or defense of his position. Imagine, however, that these varied indictments are uttered, not ad lib by many individuals but serially, by one Jew.

Let us, then, employ the old wisdom of a Western Avenue, Chicago, car salesman: "If I could, would you?" Thereby, the salesman worked to break the prospect free from a generalized sales resistance, and force him to utter a concrete (and thus potentially surmountable) objection to buying a car—for example:

SALESMAN: What is it, specifically, that you don't like?
PROSPECT: (*thinks*) Well. I don't like the color.
SALESMAN: What color would you like?
PROSPECT: (*casting about for an improbable, thus, extractive choice*) I'd only like it in light green.
SALESMAN: If I could get it for you in light green, would you buy it . . . ?

Here, the prospect, rather than reverting to an undifferentiated state of sales resistance, will utter another concrete objection.

PROSPECT: *And*, I don't like the price.
SALESMAN: What price would you like?

PROSPECT: It's a thousand dollars too high.

SALESMAN: If I could knock a thousand dollars off the price
  . . . [etc.]

The reluctant, assimilated, disaffected Jew, in my experience, is similar to this sales prospect. He will explain or excuse his apostasy with an unthought (as never challenged) blanket statement, in effect, a peremptory challenge—for example, "Zionism is criminal." We may note that this is a late-twentieth-century rendition of the historical "All Jews are business cheats" (cf. "to Jew someone down").

Here the indicted Jews are accused not of the theft of a wallet, as Fagin, or of a stock exchange, as Trollope's Melmotte, but of *an entire country*. We may note, further, that Columbus "discovered" America, but Herzl "stole" Israel. Gustav Klimt's painting of Adele Bloch Bauer, stolen from her family and heir by the Nazis, was eventually returned to her niece, Maria Altman. From the *Los Angeles Times*, 21 June 2006: "The painting is now the costliest artwork known in the world, a sensuous Gustav Klimt portrait of Altman's aunt *that the family peddled* for more than $104 million." The italics are added; but, lest any reader miss the point, the article was titled "Yours for a Price."

SALESMAN: But wait, is it a criminal act to wish to house and care for the victims of the pogroms and the Shoah?

PROSPECT: That's not why the state was formed.

SALESMAN: Why was the state formed?

PROSPECT: More important, *how* was it formed? Through theft of the lands from the Palestinians.

SALESMAN: If I could prove to you that those lands were, in the main, purchased, or won in wars, just as we find in the formation of *any other state* in history, would you relent in your indictment?

PROSPECT: But the Jews "base their claims" on a mythological document—the Bible.

SALESMAN: Well, let's wait now. Did they want the land because they are thieves, or because they are zealots? And might not your constant change of field indicate an underlying, unthought sales resistance? What might that be?

PROSPECT: I have no objection to the Jews, just to their actions.

SALESMAN: Oh. All of their actions? The actions of all Jews?

Wherein those who have participated in the exchange will remember, the argument defaults, on the part of the prospect, generally, to an indictment, not of the Jews, but of reason—that unfair advantage that the canny Jew will always take of the honest but simple "regular human being" (i.e., that imaginary Christian with whom the assimilated assumes to have thrown in his lot and who, magically, seems to have accepted it).

Here we may see the shift from the political "Zionism" (the quest for a homeland for the Jews) is a "crime" to the more generally racially malevolent "all Jews are Thieves," which is a *social* indictment, and on to the blanket, and nonspecific, therefore universally applicable "you Jews are *like that*." This, again, is the unstated conviction that the Jews, beyond desiring land and property, desire—for some unstatable reason—the overthrow of the right thinking. In this apriority we find that we are, in fact, the Devil.

I say that *all* objections to the race and religion, *as* race or religion, *by* Jews are examples of anti-Semitism and traceable back, as above, to the common and effective proposition "Jews are evil."

But how has the individual apostate Jew escaped this assumably ineradicable and universal racial taint to which he refers? *Through magic.*

The emancipated Jew has said "abracadabra," here formed as a statement of absolute renunciation, by which utterance he considers himself self-absolved of the racial taint. He has, in effect, been born again. And much good may it do him, he who may now brave the scorn of a notional "majority," while suffering from his obdurate and hurtful abandonment of his own race and culture. This obduracy is born, perhaps, in ignorance and the understandable wish for safety but allowed expression, it is matured into an arrogant treason.

You Can Just Be Nothing

> If sanity, if mental balance, as we now know depends upon the facing of reality, upon the acceptance of necessity, it is no wonder that neurotic symptoms and ill-organized lives are found among those Jewish liberals, often brilliant and cultivated persons, who withdraw from the hard fact of Jewish uniqueness into the hiding places of analogy, into the refuge of false alikeness and a hopeless community effort with other groups.
>
> —LUDWIG LEWISOHN,
> "The American Jew" (1950)

In the film *Boys Town* (1938), Mickey Rooney, the new boy, is shown the ropes by an oldster. Rooney asks about religion at Boys Town. His mentor tells him, "You can be anything, a Catholic or a Protestant." "What about if I'm nothing?" Rooney says. "Then you can just be nothing," he is told.★

Why would anyone who possessed a heritage, racial, cultural, or otherwise, prefer to "just be nothing"? Can one simply choose to embrace a negative, and must not such a choice be, effectually, a repudiation? Why would assimilated Jews (Jews by race or cultural heritage) choose to repudiate a culture, a history, and a religion about which they know nothing? For the last thing to go, the last vestige of identifiably "Jewish" characteristics is, I believe, a sense of the need for social justice—this seems to remain, self-interpreted as "humanism," or "doing good," after all other identifications with the tribe have gone.

The protest movements, from the days of civil rights to the environmentalism of the present day, are disproportionately peopled by Jews and, in fact, by *lapsed* Jews. But the racially engrained mitzvot persist, in their observance, as do-gooderism and, in their nonobservance, as guilt and anomie.

The assimilated or lapsed Jew understands the commandment (e.g., Do we oppress the stranger?) correctly as awakening anxiety in its nonperformance. He correctly associates the commandment with Judaism—his dilemma, unfortu-

---

★ Sadly, glaringly, "Skinny," the chap who instructs Mickey Rooney, is played by Martin Spellman, immediately and undeniably recognizable as a Jew.

nately, consists in his prescription: escape from Judiasm, and the sense of anomie will vanish.

But since he does not understand the anomie's source, he cannot understand its cure. For "Jewish guilt" is not a side effect of being Jewish but of being insufficiently Jewish. Buddhism will not cure it, self-help will not cure it, good works will not cure it, *A Course in Miracles* will not cure it— all of these, ranging from religion to nostrum, cannot eradicate the lapsed Jew's sense of being lost. For he *is* lost.

Perhaps five or ten more generations of nonobservance may eradicate the Jew's need to belong. Perhaps some future being may say, "You know, we have Jewish blood in our family," in the same way that a contemporary Anglo may brag "My great-great grandmother was a Cherokee"; but today we are too close to five thousand years of observance, too close to the immigrant generations, too close to the Shoah for any lapsed Jew to feel anything other than self-loathing or its Doppelgänger, arrogant assurance of his escape.

What is this specter, from which the fallen-away shrinks as from defiling a corpse—a specter so loathsome it may not be examined? It is intimacy. And let us note: Who is the new community with whom the unaligned, nonobservant, anti-Zionist ex-Jew shares his brave feelings of freedom? It is invariably a community of like-minded Jews.

The Jew will not swap tales of his own anti-Semitism with the non-Jew, as he knows that to air such beliefs is shameful. *Not* that it is a "shanda fun dem goyim" but that it is *racism.* The only protected area in which he may air his enlightenment is a Jewish one.

Here we may find the proud inheritor of millennial traditions, happy to announce that he is ignorant of all observance, happy to indict the State of Israel in ignorance of its trials, and blind to the fact that it is a *country* and, like any country, will make mistakes. This ex-Jew, like the member of any hermetic or oppressed group—gays, veterans, the disabled, etc.—will unerringly and autonomically seek out his own, with whom he may share his fantasy of individuality. This person, who likely has never felt the warmth of Shabbos, the purity of Yom Kippur afternoon, the beauty of "Eishet Chayil," who will not marvel at the courage of his immigrant grandparents, or weep at the death of his cousins in the Shoah and of his cousins on the boardwalk in Tel Aviv, confuses the ideal with the real.

He feels that, rationally, a person, as the boy in *Boys Town,* may be free to choose, to opt out of any inconvenient association, free of debt, and so of guilt. But he may not and is pursued by an unquenchable sense of loss. He may identify this loss as a desire for justice, for redress, for equality, for freedom. The sense of loss will persist. His guilt and anxiety are not for the unfortunate state of the world but for his identity.

This identity cannot exist outside the tribe. He is insulated from his desire, and the shame that his confession must entail, by identifying *the tribe itself* as that which must be shunned.

Sins of the Jews

Nothing is more dangerous, either for an individual,
or for a people, than to confess to sins of which one is
innocent.

—AHAD HA'AM

They brought it on themselves," the disaffected Jew said
to me, "by the nature of their myth. The Passover myth
is corrupt. It is a myth of chosen subjugation in the face of a
greater power."

"This," I said, "is a rather inventive interpretation of a
story which, arguably, supports the opposite view. Historically, it has signified an endorsement of self-liberation."

Nevertheless, it is an interesting diagnostic, the fellow's
drash. And, indeed, a few moments later, he, this disen-
chanted Jew, was berating Israel, the state, for, in his words,
its aggressiveness. So, here we have two universally distrib-
uted (if, arguably, inapposite in these cases) human capacities: hope and ambition. Each capacity by him is *indicted* by

the disaffected as applied to the Jews; they are disprobative epithets—the Jew is criminally passive, the Jew is criminally aggressive. The Jews are thus, not by proof, but by the mere process of indictment, excluded from the family of humankind.

This fellow, in ignorance of the tradition, and blind to the beauty of the Passover myth, concluded his diatribe by a condemnation of the victims of the Shoah (stupid sheep). But, I asked: Were the victims of Stalin's murders sheep? The Armenians under the Turks? The Sudanese? Is there not such a thing as a "victim"? That is, a guiltless, if luckless, sufferer? Or is this state available only to gentiles?

"And let us return to Israel," I said. "Do these same Jews alone possess the sinful stain of (somehow) conspiratorial passivity? Are these the same who have incited your loathing by the opposite course? By hubristically desiring, and then building, a state?"

Conjoined in a state, or stateless, the Jews are wrong. Sufficiently vile as to forfeit claim to that most perfect award of the West—the mantle of victimhood. As true victims, they are, nonetheless somehow, guilty; involved in an ongoing war, their aggressiveness is crime, their losses are their just deserts.

In the West, particularly in America, there is no higher status than victimhood. Victims are the noble savages of our day, possessing, in their innocence, no qualities other than good. We love victims.

We do not, however, pity them. For pity, as Aristotle laid

it down, is based upon a recognition of a shared, irreducible humanity, of community with the sufferer. Our sententious love of the victim, however, treats him as an object and his woes as a special, protected subspecies of entertainment.

Just as police and military stories (presented both as fiction and as news) allow us to indulge fantasies of vengeance, so sob stories (again, of both categories) give rein to the preadolescent fantasy of impregnability. The mawkish "walks for," the wearing of bracelets and ribbons indicating affinity for a particular woe, each reveals a sentimentality that could not be further removed from pity (cf. the Jewish proverb "The rich need the poor more than the poor need the rich").

These are not celebrations of concern but, rather, carnivals of gratitude in which, rather than condoling with, we effectively *thank* the victim (the poor, deluded but useful unfortunate, the sufferer of famine, tsunami, genocide, cancer, etc.). We will note that actual loss awakens observances different in kind. Ceremonies after September 11 were brief and, in the main, spontaneous outpourings of communal grief, devoid of that atmosphere of self-congratulation that characterize "walks for . . ."

But the Jews . . . the Jews . . .

Our problematical longevity taxes the world. How may we be victims if we refuse to die? How may we be pitied if we belligerently display self-sufficiency? Must not, then, historical instances of Jewish suffering be *themselves* discounted? Hence, the Shoah, recast as (a) a devilish conspir-

acy of fantasy, (b) a harsh but just sentence upon the criminally passive, (c) a deplorable ad hoc event that, in the use
made of it by conniving opportunistic Jews (the formation
of the state), must forfeit any consideration other than as a
sick stratagem.

Perhaps, though, the deplorable Western love of the victim must be eradicated, first, in the self. Perhaps a beginning
would be the resurrection of the ability to recognize race
treason.

Lies, or Teshuva

To whom is it that these Jewish apostates appeal? For surely there is an element of performance in their protestations of nonalignment. Absent from this mime of disaffection, from criticism of things Jewish, is the recollection—present in all men not self-involved—that all men recognize a lie.

That shame and awkwardness each feels when he lies is discernible; indeed, it cannot be hidden except by the truly depraved. This shamefacedness is a tribute to and a reminder of conscience. We recognize this mawkish falseness in the lies of others; no one has ever lied his way out of an obligation without being aware that his falsity was apparent.

We gauge our lies not to the understanding but to the social position of the recipient. That is, we do not craft them according to their probability but according to the *necessity on the part of the hearer to accept them.* To those to whom we are truly indebted, or whom we wish to placate or propitiate, we seldom lie at all. Not, perhaps, from good manners but from the (reasonable) fear that the price of possible discovery far outweighs any potential benefit of success.

When we are lied to by our superiors, we feel shame for them, as they have forever diminished themselves in our eyes. How much better, we think, for them to have spoken the truth, whose inconvenience, to them, however great, could never, if they knew it, compensate them for their forfeiture of our esteem.

There are societies founded on lies: the incestuous family, for example, is bound by and, in fact, defined by the constant necessity for maintaining a fiction. More benignantly, various amateur groups, of writers, painters, poets, coalesce around an unbreakable devotion to the fiction that their work has worth—adopting, by turns, the persona of the devoted student hungry for correction and the wise preceptor full of respect for the devotee of the arts. Many Reform synagogues I have visited, and whose services I have attended, share this pervasive feeling of shamefacedness.★

Formal worship may be empty of awe, but, if so, it had better be heavy on tradition. When both true reverence (yirat shamayim) and historic ritual are lacking, the mind of the individual worshipper, deprived of any legitimate outlet

★ I specify Reform not invidiously, in distinction to Orthodox or Conservative, but only as this constitutes the major range of my experience.

for devotion, *must* revert to doubt and self-protectedness. When he perceives this same reversion around him, he has but two choices: to retire or to assert.

His perseverance in the empty service, his asseveration of its worth, is, like the acceptance of a miserable marriage, the end not only of spontaneity but of any awareness of dissatisfaction that might possibly lead to a betterment of the situation.

These empty ceremonies are not the continuation but the death of Judaism, for even if the parents mime their devotion, the children are aware of the sham; they will endure as they must, but most will be reluctant to impose the tax upon their offspring, which next generation might and likely may turn against *all* things Jewish.

At Passover it is taught that the way to glory leads through shame. Shame begins with confession, and the first confession of the apostate Jew must be "I am a fraud."

For should the Jew recoil and flee, to what group can he run? Who are these enlightened creatures who would value a bold assertion of one's independence from one's race? Imagine them.

How, please, are the self-absorbed, deceitful, busy-unto-death, distracted, irreverent, and unschooled (according to your and my constant gossip) mob who make up the totality of humankind suddenly transformed into a wise council of the Just, waiting to embrace the quondam Jew who has seen the light?

What a poor, pitiable, imitation of the Christian notion of

being "born again," this fantasy of the kind world, happy to embrace the repentant Jew. And even were it true, even if the world we decry every moment as thoughtless and wrong were to reform itself according to some fantastical ur-Christian notions of inclusivity, would it, could it, be so constituted as to somehow accept not *only* the truly repentant sinner (Jew), but the counterfeit penitent we each know ourself to be?

No, this longing to belong cannot reasonably be the desire to belong to any human group—that group does not, *can*not exist; and *its appearance*—the semblance of complete mutual acceptance among prevaricators—can be mimed only by the cult, the dysfunctional, and the shamed.

That group, then, "the group of the unaligned" to which the brave disaligned Jew burns to belong, with which he wishes to share and from which he desires admiration of his individualism, his freedom of thought, can exist only if its devotion is not put to the test: it is, essentially, a group of strangers; and I suggest the *true* measure of its possible reciprocal loyalty may be determined simply by the removal of the idea of "special circumstances."

The confederation of the shamefaced can function only through a special-case definition. Members of the "writing group" may praise each other's efforts, but would not, when the meeting's done, curl up with one of their comember's books. Members of the spiritually inert shul may praise each other's monetary contributions as "true Judaism," but would they bear arms and risk life in mutual defense, God forbid, in a pogrom? And the unaligned Jew, the Jew only by an interesting quirk of heredity—that Jew who refers to his forebears much as a wealthy man might allude to an ancestor who was a horse thief—whom might he expect, whom desire, at his bedside to give and receive comfort, to hold his hand, in mutual awe, silent before the mystery?

Primitive Secret Societies

Tribal societies arouse the universal sentiments of curiosity, fear, and awe; they surround themselves with that veil of mystery so attractive to primitive minds the world over; and they appeal with ever growing power to the social and convivial aspects of human nature, to feelings of prestige and exclusiveness, and to the consciousness of the very material privileges connected with membership. . . . By the side of the family and the tribe they provide another organization which possesses still greater power and cohesion. In their developed form they constitute the most interesting and characteristic of primitive social institutions.

In communities destitute of wider social connections, such societies help to bring about a certain consciousness of fellowship and may often, by their ramifications throughout different tribes, become of much political importance. . . . Among the Korannas of South Africa, a fraternity exists whose initiates are marked by three cuts on the chest. Said one of their members to an inquirer: "I can go through all the valleys inhabited by Korannas and by Griquas, and wherever I go, when I open my coat and show these three cuts, I am sure to be well received." After a Nkimba novice has acquired the secret language and has become a full member, he is called Mbwamvu anjata, and the members in the other districts "hail him as a brother, help in his business, give him hospitality, and converse freely with him in the mystic language."

—HUTTON WEBSTER, *Primitive Secret Societies*

What if, then, the Jews were a secret society, similar in the public imagination to the Rosicrucians, the Knights Templar, the Masons, and so on?

What if admission to this secret society depended upon a profession of faith—note that that faith here must be, to a certain extent, blind—for the true benefits of membership in a secret society must be apparent only to the initiated members. So the first step for admission is faith and a protestation of faith. The next step would be, as with any secret society, a study toward mastery of its rituals and language. These, of course, would have a deeper meaning to the acolyte who believed and understood and wished to work toward self-perfection in the craft than they would to the merely curious.

The craft here, the secret society, is Judaism; the first steps of initiation, as with the Masons, would be in study of ritual and special-case language.

The first language and practice would be that of the prayer service. The language would be prayer-book Hebrew, the language of the Torah. A mastery of the same might reveal, to the novice, further avenues of study.

We note that since Judaism is not hierarchical, the acolyte, the novice, and the initiate must determine for himself, must design for himself, further stages of initiation. Having mastered sufficient biblical Hebrew, the devotee of this secret world might be inspired to pursue those advanced texts and those systems that devolved from it. He might study Aramaic in order to read the Talmud; these studies might lead toward the Kabbalah and the mystical tradition, toward responsa and the rabbinic, ethical tradition; such studies might, then, involve the study of medieval and modern Hebrew.

His zeal for further progress in this nonhierarchal secret society, Judaism, might lead to the study of Yiddish and the sociology of one thousand years of European diaspora civilization. These studies, whether of years or decades, might confirm in the student an awe of the civilization that gave him life, and a deep longing for further knowledge. He might even conclude that beyond the specific studies, of language, culture, ritual, and philosophy, lies a mystery that opens out before him the more he participates in it, the more he devotes himself to it.

Most secret societies have, at their core, the final mystery of "the secret knowledge," which is that there *is* no secret knowledge. Judaism, as a spiritual, ethical, or social practice, has at its core a mystery so deep that not only is its existence hidden from the uninitiated but its very practitioners are hated and scorned, reviled and murdered as necromancers. What is the fear the Jew engenders and that manifests itself as hatred? Perhaps it is caused by his historical, absolute, terrifying certainty that there is a God.

Superstition

Bernard Rust, the Prussian Minister of Culture, once explained in a nation-wide radio broadcast that Palestine was the crossroads of the ancient world. That here the black race of Africa, the white race of Europe, and the yellow race of Asia met and mingled to form a mongrel folk, the Jews. This gave the Jewish nation a sense of maladjustment, arising from their racial impurity. To explain this racial maladjustment, the Jewish religion with its conception of Original Sin was developed.

—DOUGLAS MILLER,
You Can't Do Business with Hitler (1941)

Each human being has a certain amount of awe that must be discharged. It can be discharged only through ritual. If he does not engage in existing religious ritual, the individual will seek out or invent other avenues for his submission to powers greater than himself. These rituals include political conventions, sports rooting, and celebrity worship.

When the individual's awe has already been cathected in the pagan (see earlier discussion), the abstract relationship of awe to religion (which is to say, to the mystery of a prime mover) may be correspondingly disparaged.

This is the situation in which the apostate Jew finds himself. He may worship wealth, fame, status, sex, physical fitness, good works, or the notion of human perfectibility, but the already-discharged awe is now unavailable to its original progenitor, and the religious urge may thus be easily overlooked or, indeed, despised.

Satan becomes abortion doctors or abortion clinics, the Evil Empire, the Christian Right, the Bush administration, godless liberals. Here the human (unacceptable thought or behavior) has been confused with the supernatural (evil incarnate).

Good may now similarly be reduced from the ideal of a perfectly moral life to the very human achievement of those goals, the nonreligious human, in his independence, cares to name as paramount: a billion dollars, a magazine cover, etc.; and the desire for godless goals culminates, in its perfection, in the desire to be omnipotent—godlike, outside of history, outside cause and effect. (For if one might, just possibly, possess one billion dollars, might one not, theoretically, possess one hundred billion dollars and, so, rule the world?)

The urge to wealth may stand in for omnipotence, the urge to fame and endless youth for immortality.

In substituting conveniently elected totems and ceremonies for their more ancient counterparts, we have become neither more rational nor more humane, merely more confused—we have replaced awe by superstition. The ceremony of circumcision is derided as savage self-mutilation, that of breast augmentation accepted as logical fulfillment of healthy individual prerogative. Plastic surgery performed in aid of self- or community propitiation is simple cosmetic alternative; that performed in aid of religion is viewed, by the enlightened, as monstrous.

But every obeisance, performance, or sacrifice the apostate finds irrational or ludicrous in religion will be found, under another name, in his daily life. The apostate might balk at consulting a rabbi as he might a soothsayer but finds it logical to consult with a "life coach." He may scoff at the notion of evil spirits, or evil inclination, but participates with a therapist in an ongoing ceremony centered in the belief that constant attendance and a ritual recitation of his wrongs will (in some unnameable, never-to-be-tested way) stave off some unnameable catastrophe (the sequel to that previous unfortunate occurrence that an unaffected individual might identify as "his own life").

The enlightened might find ludicrous the notion of a Magic Balm of Youth, yet pay outrageous sums for an inert white cream that has been suggested to reverse the aging process. One might identify as primitive the caste differences between Cohen, Levi, and Israel yet pay exorbitantly to "move up" from one model car to the next—models operationally identical, and differing only in the placement and shape of their fenders and badging.

Man is a constantly, irremediably, deeply superstitious creature—no man more than he who is assured of his absolute rationality. He may throw salt over his shoulder, knock on wood, wear the lucky golf glove, apply the cologne used only when dating, and yet feel the intellectual superior of the poor soul who goes to shul. The apostate is not an agnostic but an unconscious polytheist. Jewish monotheism is, first of all, the intent to "give it a name"—to call to the individual's attention the fact that he is *constantly* worshipping something and to ask him to consider of what his particular practice is made.

Modern life, the Shoah, the destruction of European Jewry and its traditions have vitiated the true demand of religion. The task of reform—to eliminate the taxing, to make a stringent practice of accommodation—has neared completion, but the nagging question, the essential question, the question that can be put and answered only through ritual, though less often asked, remains. It is this: instead of worshipping the wind and the water, fortune and fame, do you have the courage to stand in awe of that which gave rise to them, to you, and to your human urges?

The obscenely wealthy seek more wealth, the world-famous more fame, the powerful ultimate power, the beautiful endless youth. Whom do we see that is immune?

The thoughtful Jew might use the gift of reason, acknowledge his fears, and seek conviction. The act will not be unrewarded.

Bar Mitzvah and Golden Calf

The bar mitzvah, undertaken at age thirteen, is a survival of the puberty ordeal found in every primitive society. In the Temple Period the Jews developed from a nomadic tribe. In the Rabbinic Period a rejection of the primitive desert ordeal (the sacrifice; cf. the akedah) became an avowal of and an endorsement of rabbinic Judaism: animal sacrifice, which had replaced human sacrifice, was itself rejected. Now the child was consecrated thus: he came before the group to read from the Torah, to explicate and expound on the meaning of the text. He endorsed, by his accomplishment, not the sacrifice of wanderer-warrior-gatherer first demanded in the desert puberty ritual but the religious intellectual life necessary to the continuation of the stateless tribe in exile.

In the diaspora, in late-twentieth-century America, the meaning and the purpose of the bar mitzvah changed again. Reform Judaism had either stressed or been unfortunately taken to have endorsed the needlessness (if not the harmfulness) of ritual.

As the general level of learning of the congregants declined, the reading from the Torah itself obtained something of an echo of the original nature of ordeal: the event was understood to celebrate not the boy's matriculation into the tribe but his final (perhaps sole) obligation to it—Bar Mitzvah became a celebration of release.

Unschooled, confused, and shamefaced, the child acted out for his elders not their requirements for his preparation for manhood but their fantasy of manumission. The lad's shamefaced bar mitzvah ratified his elders' assertion that Judaism was dead.

Should any resemblance to the golden calf be lacking, we may note that, starting after the War, the American bar mitzvah became a byword for conspicuous and bizarre consumption—a celebration of the wealth of the participants. One might decry the degradation of this ceremony as a unique form of corruption, were it not that it, far from being unique, is the type of most stories in the Torah.

An examination of the bar mitzvah's degradation—and its similarity to the story of the golden calf—may reveal something of not only the nature but also the purpose of the Torah, and of its true importance to the Jews. The Torah is, among other things, a poetic and philosophic treatment of the trauma of the clan in transition from the primitive to the civilized. The immemorial legends of the desert tribe are here assembled and redacted in the light of an overriding concept: a new inspiration has been introduced (it may be called God, or monotheism), and so everything must change.

Old ways will, of course, persist. Some must be discarded, some must be altered, some must be reunderstood.

This change is recorded as the inspiration of Abraham and the struggles of his descendants, culminating in and signified by Moses. The primitive desert clan of idol worshippers becomes the sumptuous city of Pharaoh—civilization has progressed from one discrete state to another, from the nomadic to the settled—and it is time for the clan, the Jews, *to make an accommodation with the trauma.*

This is to say, there will be no new information—the new thing, civilization, literacy, agriculture, *has* transpired, and the clan has two and only two choices: it may accept this civilization unthinkingly (and, indeed, be greatly, materially rewarded for doing so, as Moses is by Pharaoh), or, it may *retain* something of the desert ways, and wisdom, and accept the constant burden of a gap between its desires and its perceptions.

The primitive man lived in an animist state. He perceived the work of the gods all around him, and in every thing. Sociologists may have called this superstition, but it was religion. It was a direct and constant connection to the Divine, and it is understood by every human being who has ever lived in extended, direct contact with the elements.

The transition from a hunter-gatherer society to agriculture and civilization destroyed an ancient connection to the gods. Under a roof and in a city, the urge to propitiate, to fear, the Powers became the urge to fear the king; fealty (and, later, patriotism) replaced clan loyalty.

The universal human urges and transitions still remained, but they were dealt with by law rather than by custom, thus their origins were forgotten. Morality, which is a reliance on conscience, replaced awe, which is the fear of God; and law, which is an attempt to instill fear of consequences, replaced morality.

As we progressed from the desert, from the immediate connection to awe, fear, lust, greed, anger (and their immediate consequences), we became, like the snake, subtle. Civilized life required and requires a great deal of self-delusion. We became rationalizing beings, as individuals and as a society, and learned to deny not only the existence of God but also the existence of the *world*, its progressions and necessities, and of human nature (or, say, the human soul).

Uncathected longings, wonder, awe, and hope are suppressed today just as at the foot of Mount Sinai, by application of the heaviest metal in the world, gold. So the golden calf, and the million-dollar bar mitzvah are an expression of the same human longing: "I cannot control the gods, I must submit," becomes "I cannot control the gods, the gods do not exist. What is all-powerful? Man. How may I control man? Through gold: I will worship gold."

The Torah, and, so, the Jews, have infuriated both the non-Jews and Jewish apostates for two thousand years because it and they, in their devotion, present proof of the possibility of a countervailing force to the inevitable social decay of man.

The Torah may be seen, and its persistent worship understood as (inter alia) a memo to humankind. "Memo: civilization, in leaving the desert and progressing from the wandering tribe, will grow. Here is a mystery: Growth is identical to decay. Each supposed advance of humankind will and must involve an abandonment of older ways and practices that linked us directly to the Divine. This is inevitable. Just as the one-child family changes forever on the birth of the second child, the world will change with each additional member. Larger groups will require different social structures; different economic conditions and invention will further remove the individual from the practices of a life lived directly in nature.

"This process is not to be decried (it is inevitable), *but neither is it to be worshipped.* Keep the nature of this process before your eyes, and you may retain a connection to that same God that was known to you in the desert."

The Torah is a record of struggle—Abraham's struggle with his idol-maker father, Jacob with the angel, Moses with Korah. The bulk of the text is a poetic record of bizarre, unfortunate, wondrous, and deplorable strife. These stories may be understood as the inner conflict of the human being, his good against his bad, and the Torah as the struggle of the group (the Jews) to discover, refine, and preserve in action a connection to God.

The end of the Chumash is the removal of the intermediary Moses, who stood between the Jews and God. Moses was a faithful but reluctant servant. He was chosen by God and pleaded other priorities. God pressed Moses into service, and Moses struggled, not only against himself, but against the Jews, who, now as then, being human, were difficult.

The apostate, the rebellious, the apikoros, the wicked son, it may be said, is that individual to whom the Torah is addressed, who is both its subject and its intended recipient. The Jews are that race who, now accepting, now dismissing it, have been saddled with a document precisely and irrefutably addressing their apostasy.

"Jewish guilt," "Jewish self-loathing," "Jewish anti-Zionism" all bear, as part of their title and their content, "Jewish."

The scoffing "ex"-Jew and the lavish "theme" bar mitzvah were not only foretold in, but are the sole subject of, the Torah.

The Poor Shul

I should like to see any power of the world destroy this race, this small tribe of unimportant people whose wars have all been fought and lost, whose structures have crumbled, literature is unread, music is unheard, and prayers are no more answered.

Go ahead destroy that race, destroy Armenia, see if you can do it, send them to the desert without bread or water, burn their homes and churches, then see if they will not last, sing and pray again.

For when two of them meet anywhere in the world, see if they will not create a new Armenia.

—WILLIAM SAROYAN

I met two wealthy Jews of my acquaintance who were visiting at a poor shul. It was Shabbos, and the rabbi was giving them the tour. The efficient cause of their inquiry was plain, as I encountered them in a classroom of fifth-graders.

They had not come for the service but to inspect the facilities for their child to whom, to their credit, they wished to impart something of his heritage. But he was not going to have it imparted at this poor shul. Their fixed expressions told the tale of their fear, and their fear was that of contagion.

The shul, again, was poor. It rented space from a Christian fundamentalist church near a freeway.

Their faces showed they'd come to the very wrong place, and my hello their panic. The man, I saw, was afraid I'd engage him in some sort of conversation, thus extending the length, and, God forbid, the consequences of his very wrong decision.

The shul, in his defense, had nothing to recommend it. Except that it was holy. And how could a casual, let alone a fearful, visitor recognize that?

All sins, the rabbis tell us, are the sin of the spies, or the sin of the golden calf.

The man had come to the shul because he had been told that it was extraordinary. To what did it owe its reputation? To the excellence of its rabbi. That's why the prospect came. But he did not hear the rabbi, and he did not watch, let alone participate in, the service, and he left in fear.

The Israelites, we are told, created the golden calf not because they doubted Moses and his connection with God but because they *believed* in it. The impending prospect of ultimate intimacy deprived them of their senses, and they reverted, forcefully and determinedly, to the limits of the known world—their act an *insistence* that nothing existed beyond their experience.

For these Israelites, *if* a god existed, and if Moses had gone up the mountain to hear God's command and to take it to the tribes—*if* this were true, those tribes would have to abandon most of the notions and behaviors that had ruled their lives and begin again with a new template. So they asserted, in an act of wish fulfillment, that it was *not* true, they did *not* believe in Moses or God, and proceeded to demonstrate their incredulity.* Their demonstration, then, the worship of the golden calf, was effectively a proof of their awe of God.

As was the visitor's flight from the poor shul. For, if the shul contained nothing but a congregation assembled to study the word of God—no marble, no gilding, just hard benches in a hot room—if this was sufficient, then, to the prospect, something was terribly wrong with his life. So, no, he concluded, it was not his life that was lacking, but the shul. How did I know?

I knew because his reaction was not polite regret at being offered something he did not, on reflection, require; his reaction was not even disappointment but politely hidden disgust.

The shul lacked even the most basic amenities—

---

* Cf. determined serial sexual misadventures prior to marriage—each ending in an assertion that true, sustainable intimacy is impossible.

maintenance, let alone opulence—and the display of plaques commemorating donors. What was the message? That wealth, here, was pointless. Financial support might be welcomed, but wealth was not worshipped.

What advantage, then, to this successful man? Only the possibility of communion with the Divine.

See also, the bachelor who manages to find in every potential mate something just a little bit wrong. This person may be accused of, and may in fact grudgingly admit to, that malady called fear of commitment, but that may be more truthfully characterized as greed.

The perennial bachelor is afraid not of commitment but of passing up any opportunity for unlicensed sex—he is afraid not of commitment but of restraint.

The fellow shopping for a good shul may have continued his search and found that organization whose best claim was that it would make no claim on his spirit. One can imagine his gratitude and its expression in monetary donation. Which is why the great shul he visited was poor.

A Rich Shul and a Poor Shul

Poverty becomes a Jew, like a red bridle a white horse.

—Traditional

The small, alternative storefront shul, or shteibl, attracts congregants through the power of the rabbi and the rabbi's teaching. Should attendance outstrip capacity, or should the shul attract a bequest, it may trade cramped, Spartan quarters for more luxurious digs.

Suppose it has grown prosperous enough to build its own facility. It will acquire, thus, a larger staff, both to maintain the results of and to increase the size of the endowment. Where once one dealt chiefly with the rabbi, congregants now will deal more frequently with the staff.

As the bureaucracy solidifies (that is, as the congregation grows habituated to what are now seen as the legitimate rewards of prosperity), the rabbi has two choices: he or she may spend more time in administration, or "give the staff its head. In either case, the rabbi's ability to perform the original task (instruction and spiritual care) ebbs. Increased time in administration means, of course, less time for pastoral duties; resignation of such administration to the staff will eventuate, of necessity, in the shul, taking a course of its own, different from that desired by its one-time captain, the rabbi.

In the second instance, the rabbi may find his or her energies devoted not to direction but to correction of the above-indicated modifications. In either case, the rabbi's strength must ebb.

The shul may continue to prosper as the rabbi ages, but the rabbi must, of course, eventually weaken to the point of complete resignation, die, or retire. Now the staff may inherit a financially healthy system unencumbered by commitment to the actual, taxing practices of the clergy.

The founder's vision no longer exerts the drain upon its energies that was found so enervating in his or her final days, and the staff is free to devote itself to what may now be proclaimed as not only its true, but its sole, calling: administration. Having pride of place, the staff (along with its allies, the board) will be powerful in exerting direct or indirect influence in choosing the rabbi's successor. (For the board, in its newfound freedom from the more rigorous demands of religion—study, contemplation, good deeds, etc.—*must* consider the will of the standing bureaucracy in its choice of a new rabbi. For the board, being made up of business people, recognizes that the shul may function, for a while, with an uncongenial rabbi, but will fail immediately without the staff.)

The board and the bureaucracy, again, freed by the rabbi's death, absence, or senescence, will choose, or steer the congregation toward, the innocuous—that is, toward an individual successful at, thus devoted to, those things at which the staff and the board excels, such as fund-raising, consensus, and public relations. With the installation of the new, the bureaucrats find themselves in complete power. The yetzer hara, so long maligned by the religious, has been freed and exercises itself under the name of "long-established sound business practices."

Devoted, now, solely to "growth," the congregation grows. And its now-regnant bureaucrats must themselves acquire dependents. These are both the symbol of corporate success and, notionally, a shield or protection against the (real or potential) demands of the outer world (which is to say, the congregation) for those services once provided by the rabbi, such as teaching, counseling, and guidance. Now, should the actual rabbi still live, he or she may be offered an emeritus (powerless) position—useful to the corporation as a sop or distraction to any members of the once-poor shul who wonder at its degeneration. A large part of the work of this new infrastructure will be to identify this degeneration as "growth." This blandishment will attract a new membership to the congregation, one interested in cleanliness, modernity, sound accounting principles, and, thus, repelled by the irrational (e.g., religion). The influx of new congregants will solidify the gains of the bureaucrats and suggest further growth. Now those dependents hired to support and isolate the forces of corporate responsibility will have served their apprenticeship. They will, naturally, long for advancement. They will turn their heads to gaze up the corporate ladder, and their avidity will not be unremarked. Factions will be formed, and a struggle must ensue, thus signaling the advent of a terminal bureaucracy—two opposed groups warring for possession of the husk that once housed a healthy organism. The shul, then, like the rabbi, has two choices: grow and die, or resist growth and die. Only in the latter, however, may be found the possibility of a continuation of the inspired rabbi's teaching.

Happiness and Maturity

> The best I could come up with was that during my
> time in America I'd lived pretending to myself that
> the non-Jews didn't really think I was a Christ-
> killing, world-dominating, media-controlling kike—
> pretending to myself that they really didn't chide
> my Jewishness behind my back.
>
> —ALAN KAUFMAN, *Matches*

Just as (in the view of the Christians) Christianity superseded Judaism; so the contemporary Jew may long to cast
off that which he (consciously or unconsciously) understands as an outdated system of allegiance. This confused
Jew may aspire to join in that which he understands as a
more modern, non-Jewish confraternity, entry into which
will more fully integrate him into society at large, thus
bringing happiness.

He is, here, twice deluded. First, the state of perfect,
relaxed integration that he ascribes to the non-Jews, their

absence of anomie and anxiety, is a fiction. (*If* the non-Jewish, that is, the majority view of society is less anxiety-provoking at all, it is in the majority's freedom to look at the notion of the perfect state and recognize it as a fantasy.)

Second, this integration the Jew supposes his Christian brothers enjoy—just beyond the borders of his own unfortunate (spiritual or racial) segregation—*should* it exist, the Jew would, in fact, be debarred from it because of his race. So we may find the apostate miming belief in a system or society whose imperfection is perfectly evident to all observant individuals who do not have a vested interest in fantasy.

The apikoros is in love with a fiction that, if it existed, would exclude him. His delusion of freedom to choose sentences him to a life of disappointment. The cause of this disappointment is, as is normal in us all, identified as "someone else." Psychiatry allows the individual to identify the cause of this unrest as one's parents and the cause of bigotry as another race; Jewish self-loathing allows the practitioner to combine both.

The happier individual, rather than investing in his own woes and casting about for their *insoluble cause* (a lapsed childhood, a genetic enormity), will turn his attention toward their solution. This individual, the apostate Jew, might say of his anomie, "I feel Jewish guilt," "Jewish anxiety," or "Otherness." But these attributions lead toward no change and only guarantee his continued, worthless, self-awarded prerogative of recrimination. The moment the individual takes responsibility for his own state (which is to say, upon maturity), he must and will reinvestigate the belief system that previously had linked *operationally* associated misery with inaction.

The question, then, might arise: why have I been investing in unhappiness and calling it "Jewishness"? It might occur to him that if Judaism, or "Jewishness," is actually inert (as he sometimes holds), it is irrational for him, still, to be complaining about either its practices or its deficiencies. If, on the other hand, it is operational in his life, in what ways does his disdain differ from racial prejudice?

Sadomasochistic Phenomena; or, the Two Chelms

[I]n masochistic perversion sexual satisfaction is arrived at by being humiliated, enslaved, or physically ill-treated; . . . in masochistic fantasies the imagination of similar situations leads to masturbation.

—KAREN HORNEY,
"Masochistic Phenomena" (1937)

The masochistic and sadistic imagination engages in fantasies wherein the cryptosexual delight of unlimited power is experienced (equally and perhaps interchangeably) as victim and perpetrator.

Holocaust films and slave epics are, essentially, these sexual fantasies. Their viewer is permitted, by the rectitude of the innocent sufferer's cause, to engage in fantasies of submission, simultaneously enjoying fantasies of dominance.

But it is all too possible for the participant to confuse the mythic-neurotic archetype with a real group coincidentally bearing the same name. We know that in Eastern Europe there were two Chelms: the one a repository of the world's most ignorant creatures;* the other, an actual small town in Russia-Poland.

There are, similarly, two Palestines and two Israels. And to many, the fantasy Palestinians: totally wronged, totally powerless, offers the masturbatory fantasy of a mythic race so put-upon that they are empowered, limitlessly, to kill.

This fantasy, just as the fantasy of (as opposed to the actual) Holocaust, allows the devoted to indulge in the simultaneous sadism and masochism: the Palestinians are wronged and, so, empowered. They kill with suicide bombs and are, thus, unstoppable; their death, along with their murder, is endlessly sad, as they have been driven by their sufferings to the ultimate extremity.

This engagement with the mythic (as opposed to the real) Palestinians allows—and, as Bernard Lewis has pointed out, is, in all too many cases, confected to allow—an otherwise permitted race-hatred: anti-Semitism.

Anti-Semitism is a profoundly sexual fantasy—a sado-masochism founded on religious or pseudoreligious (e.g., Marxist or Nazi) views, which views are variously called "social" or "racial." It is (consider the bizarre paraphernalia of the Nazis, the impossibly intricate illogic of the Holo-

---

* The butt of numerous jokes told by Jews about archetypally foolish people.

caust denier) a fantasy capable of being worked out end-lessly in everyday life: quite literally, a dream come true.

It was, and is, as was the case with the American chattel slavery, a dream addending to faith and sexuality the induce-ment of financial gain: In America, free slave labor; in the Holocaust, Jewish possessions (indeed, down to the gold in the victims' teeth, their hair, and meal made from their bones; and, today, the State of Israel.)* How can one under-stand this frenzy called reason?

Only as dementia.

The opposite of this hidden and less-hidden Jew-hatred is not philo-Semitism—this is and would be an equally false and degrading patronization. (Cf. "diversity" programs in American schools, calculated to "expose" the children of affluent whites to the somehow magically cleansing or edu-cative capacities of what, if truth be told, they must hold to be those "noble savages," those of darker-colored skin.) Philo-Semitism in the eyes of the world could be brought about (may God forbid) only by the destruction of the State of Israel, and the reemergence of the archetypal Jew as Victim.

---

* For, let us note that the State of Israel, a legally constituted entity formed, like many states, by and under United Nations Charter and defended since its inception by the universally acknowledged right of national Arms, is deemed by many supposedly right-thinking individuals, Arab and Western, as a simple vail of those who'd like to appropriate it. The State is, in this view, a prerequisite not different from the Jewish bones of the victims of the Nazis' ovens.

If the Jew is not a victim but merely a human being, the sadomasochistic fantasy of murder- and (self-) forgiveness cannot be played out and the obscene pornographic drama of anti-Semitism is stifled before the final, ejaculatory moment. The unwillingness of real Jews to die in cooperation with this sick, masturbatory fantasy of anti-Semitism further inflames the psychotic bigot as it brings his fantasy into relief. Here the Jew has offended not only in myth but in reality.

Imagine the infantile thrill in saying there exists an iniquity so vast that one may, if one is its victim, perpetrate, indeed, delight in, the murder of schoolchildren, of families at prayer, of the elderly: an iniquity so vast that one may condone every instance of what (did the case not involve Jews) must be an "excess," by bemoaning, not with resignation but with sympathy, the death of Palestinian children "forced," not by their parents, but by their neighbors, to kill themselves)—the fantasist, again, thus coupling bloodlust to self-exoneration.

There were two Chelms, and there are two Middle Easts. The true Middle East is involved, as it has been throughout history, in a territorial dispute. This dispute involves Jews.

The Middle East of fantasy offers not two groups of human beings endeavoring to sort out a tragedy but one group of human beings and a group of Jews.

The armchair Marxists, Holocaust deniers, anti-Semites, and other propounders of the "special case" will not forgo the sick sexual pleasure of these fantasies. Those of clearer vision and goodwill may see, in these fantasies, the permitted, vicious, and boundless license for hatred engendered by the mythic identification of not one but two subhuman groups: the world-conquering Christ-killing Jews, and the powerless perfect-victim Palestinians, who know no better than to murder their own young.

Ritual

Ours is an ailing society. There is much gratification and striving toward gratification but little joy.

The absence of joy is compensated for by aggression and greed. "Perhaps," the unhappy think, "I can find joy in appropriating that which belongs to someone else." The Jewish tropism toward assimilation is, in large part, a race-specific example of the more generalized contemporary American greed, which is the wish for *more*, the deeper meaning of which is the wish for *better*, or change.

But lunacy may be defined as the compulsion to repeat the same action in response to the same stimulus and wish for a different result.

The assimilated Jew, whether conscious of the drive or not, muddles toward community and calls it yoga, self-help, agnosticism, Buddhism, sports participation or rooting, in much the same way as the wealthy try, serially, this or that new car, home, husband, or wife. Each initially exciting new choice, of course, pales with familiarity, as it was not the previous toy that was deficient but the individual's understanding of his own needs. The lack is not in his choice but in his obsession—in himself.

Why would he, the wicked son, discard his heritage, his religion, his race, and his natural community? What does he actually hope to gain by his supposed freedom?

The Jewish word for apostate is *apikoros*, a corruption of the Greek name Epicurius, whose philosophic school held that the highest good was to choose, unfettered by prejudice or tradition, among the good things the world has to offer. If this is, as he holds, the highest good, why is the apikoros miserable?

If this belief is truly held, why is he driven to seek ratification for his unalignment? And why does he seek it *exclusively* from similarly disaffected Jews?

This is the case of the autonomic attempt at creation of community. But he builds not upon the rock of their shared heritage but upon the fiction of their freedom—like children playing at running away, miming their independence, *of necessity* under the protective gaze of those committed to their safety.

Anomie is the sickness of the American Age—the feeling of rootlessness, of purposelessness, colored over by the vehement assertion of freedom (whatever that may mean), and the unstated but essential implication that this freedom confers, upon the nation and individual, some unnameable preeminence. We find this cant of freedom (which is to say, preeminence) in the mouths of corrupt politicians wishing to incite and inspire—fettered by the absence of ideas, reduced to the recitation of magical chants.

The American Jew is not exempt from the general malaise, but he may be tasked with an additional burden. If he is ignorant of his people and their ways, he may attribute a generalized cultural disaffection to his own particular situation, thus exacerbating both the actual problems attributable to his situation as an American and to his situation as an uncommitted Jew. This ignorance, this inability to correctly understand a generalized social problem, may metastasize into apostasy.

In our contemporary society, ceremonies of matriculation (which is to say, societal endorsement and thus amelioration of the problems of maturation) are, in the main, absent, corrupt, optional, or moot. These ceremonies, where they still exist, are subject to discount by the unbeliever, the disaffected, the intellectual. His assertion of "freedom" from that which he sees as compulsion, however, may be understood as strengthening rather than weakening the case for observance.

Healthy societies recognize that transition, birth, death, manhood, womanhood, marriage, grief require a mechanism that will *force* the affected to submit to change. The ritual—bar mitzvah, baptism, marriage, military induction, Kaddish—removes from the individual the corrosive, indeed, *destructive* element of choice.

For what individual would, willingly, surrender the known

state and privileges of childhood, bachelorhood, civilian life for the unknown and most likely arduous responsibilities and duties of a more demanding state?

The healthy society rips the matriculant from the old state and debars him from reentry. If the new state is optional, if the progress toward it is reversible, the individual is left with a constant anomie, and he may, likely, identify its cause as the more mature state itself; and malign both it and the fact of ceremony in general. The widespread Western derogation of ritual further exacerbates the apostate's disaffection and endorses his indulgence in flight.

The times are against him. What is for him?

A six-thousand-year-old tradition that recognizes his dilemma.

The Apikoros and Gun Control; or *The Oslo Syndrome*

There is a statistic floating around for sufficient time as to have had its origins, and thus its probability attain the force, if not of fact, then of conventional wisdom: a firearm, kept in the house for self-protection is X times more likely to injure its owner than to injure an intruder.

Let us set aside the statement's probability and examine it philosophically. Let us, in fact, suppose that it is true. A home owner is more likely to be protected by the *absence* of a gun than by the *presence* of a gun. Why? Or, differently, the gun in the hand of a malefactor is an irresistible tool of aggression, but the same instrument, with the same potential, in the hands of the law abiding is not only ineffective, but injurious.

The old joke has a man-in-the-street reporter asking passersby for the greatest scientific advancement of all time; one says space travel, one says atomic energy, and another the thermos. Why the thermos? "Well," the man responds, "you put in coffee, it keeps it hot; you put in lemonade, it keeps it cold." "*So?*" the reporter asks, and the man responds, "How does it *know*?"

How does the gun know the worth of the person holding it? Let us suppose that this same malefactor and gunslinger took the gun home after a night of depredations and he is awakened from his sleep by a burglar. Would the gun in *his* house be more apt to inflict harm on him than on the burglar?

I believe most would respond "No." Why?

"How does it know?"

For the gun, like the thermos, is neutral. It is inert unless and until wielded by a human being.

If the burglar may master the (fairly simple) rudiments of gun safety, but the ordinary citizen is debarred, we might ask, "Debarred by what?" And we might answer that the absolute belief in remaining unarmed is not a wish to *court* harm but a wish to *avoid* it—that the propitiatory identification with the aggressor is believed *more* effective than self-assertion.

If we substitute assimilated Jew for gun-adverse home owner, the otherwise bizarre urban myth may come into focus. (And it is not, I think, out of place to remark that repetition of this absurd notion of the effectiveness of surrender is most often in the mouths of Jews. It is mouthed as a recognition symbol—a hailing sign of membership in the group of right-thinking urban liberals; its psychological underpinnings are, and, I believe, are recognized—if only subconsciously—as anti-Semitic, anti-Zionist: "Self-protection incites violence.")

How odd that these same middle-aged, intellectual Jews, who asked their parents of the Shoah, "Why didn't they fight *back*?" have adopted, in their maturity, that same passivity that they, as children, attributed (wrongly) to their race.

I have never heard this "keeping a gun is more likely . . ." statistic from anyone but a Jew. It is never presented as a rational, individual decision—"I would rather risk home invasion, murder, and rape than chance inflicting damage on my family through my own negligence"—but always as a statement of *faith*—"The decision is not *mine*, I merely submit, happily, to its authority."

The authority, here, of the statistic and the authority of the burglar are one: They are that which one is powerless to oppose. They are that society of the Irresistible Other—the liberal, Jewish voice of the *New York Times*, of National Public Radio, the right-thinking, Jewish Left, which seeks the illusory solidarity of identification with the illusory, inert, supposedly moral, wider world—which is to say with (in their view) the non-Jewish world.

This is the blame-the-victim mentality that asked, after September 11, "What *could* we have done to make those people so angry? Should we not examine ourselves?" This is the convinced rectitude of the friend who asks the cancer victim what she did to "welcome the disease."

What is the source of this idiotic, immoral cant?

In *The Oslo Syndrome*, Kenneth Levin wrote: "What motivates those Jews who are active in or align themselves with these various Israel-indicting bodies . . . ? . . . a wish to believe, in the face of anti-Jewish pressures, that Jewish salvation can be obtained by embrace of a wider identity of leftist acolyte and by Jewish self-reform and self-effacement in conformity with leftist tenets."★

Here, in abandonment of Jewish heritage, solidarity, and religion, the apikoros posits a confraternity of the reasonable and then insists on inhabiting it, in spite of all evidence to the contrary of its nonexistence, preferring the irrationality *and, indeed, the danger* of his actual, unprotected position to the danger to his psyche of the truth: that he is a Jew, that the world is not fond of the Jews, and that his only *chance* of safety lies with the Jews.

It is not the gun in the home that causes his umbrage, but his panic at facing his real position. The benefits, indeed, the delights, of his race and its heritage might very well outweigh his panicked drive to assimilate, *if* they were known to him.

Perhaps these unseen benefits are denied, in fact viewed with repugnance, as their embrace might reveal to him his cowardice.

★ Kenneth Levin, *The Oslo Syndrome, Delusions of a People Under Siege* (Hanover, N.H.: Smith & Krause, 2005).

Racism

Voters:

The Jews loom large only because we are on our knees.

RISE UP!

Fifty thousand reap the benefit of the hopeless labor wrung out of thirty million French—their trembling slaves.

It is not a question of religion—THE JEW is of a different race—the enemy of our own.

JUDAISM: Voilà the Enemy!

In standing for election I give you the opportunity to protest, with me, against the Jewish Tyranny.

Do so—it is a question of Honor.

—From a French broadside, A. WILLETTE,
standing for election to the legislature, 1889

Having experienced racism as a racist makes its appearance and operation much clearer. I grew up in a time of separate drinking fountains.

The lie of black inferiority was so pervasive that to the child it must have been true. So that, in opposition to reason, morality, observation, experience, and common sense, I considered blacks somehow inferior.

In what did this supposed inferiority consist?

I knew, my young self, that they were human beings, that they were no different intellectually, or physically, than the spectrum of nonblacks. But yet they must be inferior, or I, or else the world and I, must necessarily have been involved in a vicious, sick delusion.

But yet I, who considered myself intelligent, and acceptably humane and moral, thought blacks, in some magical way, were inferior to whites. The rhetoric of "Can't you *see* . . . ?" would avail nothing and, in fact, reinforced, to my depraved mind, the delusion.

For the rhetoric came, to my mind, from supplicants, which is to say, inferiors.

I count myself greatly privileged to have lived long enough to see the beginning of the end of racism in this country. It is not my place to speak of the benefits to the oppressed. It is difficult and, indeed, pointless to make an endorsement that would be paternalistic—one might as well confess a righteous content at a fall in the murder rate—but I have benefited personally. I am better off without this sick delusion, as are my children, as is the body politic in which I live. An increased clarity aids me in recognizing this delusion in others: notably in the reaction of much of the Christian West, and of its press, to the State of Israel.

The bombings of southern black churches could and can under no possible ethical system be excused. These crimes can, by rational beings, be considered as nothing other than monstrous murder. But the bombings of Jews in Israel by terrorists suggest, to otherwise rational minds, that "the other side deserves a fair hearing."

Why this exception? Because the Palestinians use their own children to carry the bombs? The Japanese acted similarly with their kamikazes, yet no one thought their actions increased the rectitude of their cause.

Depraved individuals in the West have killed their own children,★ yet no one considers the murderers' cause just because the children were their own. Is not the murder of their own children, if not more reprehensible than the murder of the children of others, then at least equally so?

That the Palestinians want land from the State of Israel, does this excuse the murder of the Jews? Then why not ask of the bombers of New York, and of their cronies, to list their demands, so that we may better understand and, perhaps, reward them.

Terror is terror. Everywhere except in Israel. We are going to war with Iraq, with Al Qaeda, but not with the Hamas, a representative of which issued in the early years of this millennium a plea that the world not consider his people

★ E.g., the Jonestown massacre.

terrorists, since they bombed only because of the ongoing situation with Israel. In effect, they only killed Jews. Murdered vacationers in Kenya are not vacationers but Jews, which is to say, "other than human beings," and there we have the unfortunate truth:

The "Rich Jews" somehow want to take over the world.

The "Poor Jews" want to take over the settlements.

The Jewish financial interests want to bleed the earth.

The Jewish financial interests, somehow, for some reason, want to destroy the world economy.

Palestinian terrorists murder their own children, and the world blames the Jews.

I am coeval with the State of Israel. I was born November 30, 1947.

In my lifetime we Jews, mythologically, have served the cause of soft pornography. The world weeps at our being killed. What fun.

I wrote, years ago, that Holocaust films are "*Mandingo* for Jews," and that the thrill, for the audience, came and comes from a protected indulgence of anti-Semitism: they get to see us killed and to explain to themselves that they feel bad about it.

The film *The Sum of All Fears* has Tom Clancy putting the world itself at the brink of chaos because the dumb Jews have misplaced one of their atomic bombs. Further, as the film progresses, we find that the plutonium for the bomb was stolen from the United States. Where does the blame accrue?

Plucky little Belgium struggles against the Hun, but not Israel. Well.

What can we do? I believe we can do this: we can speak up. Many of us harbor fantasies about speaking up against the Nazi tyranny. How could the world not have spoken in 1933, in 1943, we ask? Were I alive then, we fantasize, I would have spoken. . . .

But we were not, or not of an age of reason, and we cannot "speak up" in the past. We can speak up *now*.

Don't let an instance of anti-Semitism pass. Stand up for yourself, and stand up for your people. It is possible to support the Palestinian cause without being an anti-Semite, and there are people of goodwill who do so. But much of the pro-Palestinian feeling in the West is a protected example of anti-Semitism, and, when and as it is such, it should be opposed.

Performance and Restraint

"All development is weaning."

—DR. DONALD GAIR, M.D.

One may approach or attempt to propitiate a mystery through performance. One may also do so through restraint. This is the great lesson of the Akedah.

One may worship God through sacrifice, through scarifying of the flesh, through prostration, and one may worship God through that respect evidenced by restraint: have no false god, have no idols, do not mix milk and meat.

Those commandments Judaism qualifies as "negative," the " 'not' commandments"—don't kill, don't steal, don't bear false witness—are of immediately apparent utility. Among the negative commandments are also those whose utility is, perhaps, more abstract, e.g., don't have sex during menstruation, don't work on the Sabbath, don't mix milk and meat, silk with wool.

These, at a minimum, may remind the observant that he

is not God, that there exists a power greater than he, his desires, or, indeed, his intellect and that submission to that power is a first step toward communion with it.

Similarly, one may gain inclusion in a group through performance or through restraint. The performance of ritual may be the attempt to gain the attention, and thus the approbation, of some greater power. This power may be a deity, a religion, or some organization that claims to represent such.

The rituals of baptism, circumcision, the Hadjj are all survivals of the notion of ordeal. The ordeal here has been abstracted, but the underlying idea is clear: suffering, pilgrimage, ritual purification, trial by water will attract the notice of the gods and of their representatives.

The undergoing of ordeal answers the central question both of the religious acolyte and of the victim of the confidence man: "Why me?" For the ordeal, presenting itself as an attempt to impress the gods, is, to the contrary, an attempt to impress the acolyte. His successful conclusion of the ritual instills in him the naturally occurring suspicion that perhaps, in his acceptance, the group has made a terrible mistake.

We note that the individual, by *accepting* the power of ritual, endorses the power of, and thus feels himself worthless before, the mystery the ritual bids to serve (the ritual thus essentially substituting its own concerns for a generalized anomie) and that increasing devotion to the religious group may address this anxiety and, so, awaken in him increasing gratitude—called, variously, filial piety, patriotism, religious dogmatism, or sports rooting.*

So much for ceremonies of performance.

Ceremonies of restraint are more problematic because, although they may propitiate the gods, they, being in the nature of a nonevent, may seem, to the individual, less effective in propitiating the group.

The problem is, of course, circumvented by the *vow*, by its proclamation, and by outward demonstrations thereof: the nun's habit, the Amish dress, *payot*, and, perhaps, thinness (considered as a representation to the group of the individual's power of self-control).

But there is another category of restraint—that which, in *rejection* of certain ritual practices, defines the individual as a member of a differing group. Such observances, while not identifying the individual to the group (not taking the Lord's name in vain, for example), nonetheless create unit cohesion by stilling the individual's anxiety about his own self-worth—and through his subsequent ascription of this freedom to the group and its desiderata.

"Yes," he may think, "I am and deserve to be a member of that wise group, A, and am assured both of my inclusion and

---

* This is why one sees half-naked fans shivering in the subzero weather of the football stadium—autonomically re-creating themselves as ritually purified priests, capable of interceding for the sports team before the sports' god. They perform a hieratic display of suffering that might not only sway the gods, but banish from the performers the terrible notion of their own worthlessness vis-à-vis the actual combatants.

of its worth, as I discover the power to restrain myself as instructed, from the abhorrent practices of that vile group, B." And, consequently, perhaps, not, "Am I good?" but "Obviously, then, I am good, and my group is good because it practices restraint. Perhaps, then, it possesses *other* excellences, not perceptible to the outsider. Perhaps I shall investigate them."

The power of restraint, thus, is that of *self-suggestion*. It is not that the previously unaligned individual's thought processes have been changed; rather they have been *subverted*.

Today the young wish to get tattooed. By such they indicate their ability to undergo ordeal, and, by such, and its concrete sign, they distance themselves from parental control.★

Jewish tradition forbids the scarring of the flesh and tattooing. The Jew who wishes to permanently decorate his body is in the same position as the Jew who decides to opt out of his religion. He feels, in a state that I think may fairly be described as "adolescent," the longing to belong, to indi-

---

★ Most cosmetic plastic surgery, similarly, while presenting itself as the individual's attempt to gain or retain membership in a group from which he or she is physically debarred (the young, the beautiful) is, actually, a proclamation of ordeal. The patient, here, undergoes physical alteration not in an attempt to "remain young" but in an attempt to conquer the shame of his or her exclusion. "See," the facelift testifies, "though I am no longer young, this painful procedure proves that I have not lost my devotion to the group. I am, indeed, willing to be disfigured in respect for what, to me, are its now unobtainable ends."

viduate himself from his parents and those years of their onerous control. He longs to join the wider world, which in his ignorance he identifies as "that which does not pertain to my parents." He then physically himself as a ritual of individuation.

Well and good. But what if that outlet were *denied* him? What if tattooing were viciously punished, or fatal? If so, he might be forced to face and so to understand and perhaps deal with the longing the conventional expression of which was denied him.

He might, then, ask "*Why* do I wish to be tattooed? Why is it unimportant to me that, though my tastes may change, my tattoo will remain? Is it truly possible to distinguish myself and proclaim my individuality by doing the exact same thing as all of my peers?" Thus, perhaps, "Is there a happier, a more exclusive, a more attractive group to which I might aspire than the mere confederacy of the tattooed?"

These ruminations, prompted by restraint, might reveal to the questioner something surprising, unsuspected, and perhaps useful about that time of transition in which he finds himself. This process of thought, then, might be a *true* period of matriculation, these mental and spiritual ruminations *themselves* an ordeal of change, whose worth (as opposed to that of the tattoo) might grow over time. And this period of restraint might bear fruit over time in the choices that might proceed from it.

The apostate Jew, the wicked son, similarly, bears the

curious double longing: to individuate himself and to be an individual worthy of inclusion in a group—to feel self-worth.

Ignorant of the practices of his own tribe, he gravitates toward those he considers Other: other than his parents, his race, his religion—thinking, as does the adolescent, that they possess some special merit (that they are not his parents).

But these new groups are attractive to the apostate merely because they are foreign. In his attraction to them, he thinks, as does the adolescent, that he has discovered a special, magic stratagem: "I may simply *flee!*"

The urge to belong is real; it is strong; it is, in most, irresistible.

But imagine if this adolescent being ratifies the urge but reconsiders its expression. What if he exercises restraint? What if he denies himself the undeniable urge to leave, to gash his flesh, to be the Other, to flee the tribe? He will, then, be confronted with those feelings he has feared and suppressed, which are his deepest desires.

He may then perceive the true, the natural, the inevitable nature of his longing, which is simply to belong, and may, in this period of restraint, reason further, why not study how to belong to the tribe that is his own?

Dead Jews and Live Jews

"Don't forget you must pitch the old black male vs. the young black male, and the young black male against the old black male. You must use the dark skin slaves vs. the light skin slaves, and the light skin slaves vs. the dark skin slaves. You must use the female vs. the male, and the male vs. the female."

—From the Willie Lynch Letter, a speech purportedly given in 1712 in the colony of Virginia by a British slave owner from the West Indies, on the subject of subjugation★

Well," the old lefties said, "we just discovered correspondence between Anne Frank's father and the U.S. Department of State. He was, it seems, begging the United States for those documents that would allow him and his family to immigrate. And he was, of course, denied."

★ Quoted from *The Willie Lynch Letter and the Making of a Slave* by Kashif Malik Hassan-el (Chicago, Lushena Books, 1999). I am indebted to Ving Rhames, who brought the Lynch letter to my attention.

We shook our heads. This was a familiar form of communion between Jews of our age—I was born right after the War; they were born in the thirties. We all had either relatives of some degree of consanguinity, or friends of relatives, who had died in Europe. We all knew Jews with the camp tattoos on their left arms, and the murder of the European Jews was to us a living, ineradicable memory.

One of the members of our group had fled from Warsaw in September of 1939, her family strafed by the Luftwaffe on the roads out of Poland.

In the 1970s and '80s, we talked of our fears for America in the midst of a period of radical change, and dinner talk progressed pleasantly, and familiarly, as might have been predicted. And then my friends continued their—our—harangue against the administration with an indictment of their position on Israel.

"And how can they support the Israelis over the Palestinians and call themselves champions of freedom?" they wondered. "The two-state solution is the only answer."

"But," I said, "the Palestinians have vowed to drive the Jews into the sea. A two-state solution would mean the end of Israel."

And they shrugged, meaning "Let the chips fall where they may."

"Do you realize," they said, "the indignities to which the Palestinians are subjected by this new wall?"

I nodded.

"They are forced to wait hours to travel from their homes to their jobs."

I responded that many Israelites did not have that problem, because they were dead, killed by suicide bombers, killed in their buses on the way to school. My friends shrugged again.

"The problem," they said, "is Israel itself. Do you know, do you know that Ben-Gurion said that Israel was settled by 'the scum of the camps'?"

"What does that mean?" I said.

They explained that Ben-Gurion's view and *their* view was that the only Jews who escaped the camps were those who had sufficient criminal instincts or talents to sell out their like, to collaborate with the Nazis, and, thus, live to freedom.★

I thought this was the worst comment I had ever heard— vicious race treason, the leftist equivalent of the most rabid rantings of the know-nothing Right. My friends had adopted the Jacobin rhetoric of the suicide bombers, directed not only against humanity, but particularly against their own people.

Their idea of a Jew, then, was Anne Frank. Why? Because she was dead. She could, in failure, be accorded merit, but, *had she lived*, had she and her family survived, they would

---

★ I can nowhere find this phrase expressed by Ben-Gurion and cannot imagine him uttering it.

have been guilty of a crime against humanity, to wit, having survived.

The only good Jew was, in effect, a dead Jew.

Now, my Jewish friends—how were *they* exempt? They had lived through the War but bore no taint. Through what personal excellence had they survived?

Had their immigrant parents delayed their European emigration by some scant years, my friends would have died in the camps, and yet they felt themselves free to anathematize the survivors. This was not survivor guilt but cowardice; it was preemptive treason. They were selling out, in advance, their like.

There was, of course, an element of self-reassurance in their stance—that such could never befall them. But *why*? Because they were intellingent? Because they were *bold*? They were neither; because they were "Jewish but not *that* Jewish."

The Holocaust, to them, was not tragic but intellectually inconvenient.

Who is this savant who blames the victim? Who is this immune individual who asks, as does the Wicked Son, "What does all this mean to *you*?"

Who are these vile friends on the Left, who enjoy and applaud themselves for enjoying the quirks, customs, and observances of every race and culture but their own? They are a plague.

They are the Korah Rebellion, turning against Moses; they are the generation of the desert, worshipping the golden calf, and they are the spies who would not enter Canaan.

The rabbis, again, teach that all sin is essentially that of the golden calf, or that of the spies.

In the first, the Jews are awaiting Moses' descent from the mountain with the word of God. Overcome by the imminence of revelation, terrified of loss of autonomy, guilty with the burden of their own sinfulness, and loath to cease sinning, they set up a golden bull calf and worship it. They award themselves the ability to *create* a God, in effect, in order to *become* God. This is the sin of idolatry.

Later, Moses sends twelve scouts to spy out the Promised Land. They report that it flows with milk and honey but that it is unfortunately guarded by giants, against whom the Jews could not possibly prevail. This attitude infects the Jews, who are, then, kept out of the Promised Land until the coward generation of the desert dies. This is the sin of discouragement, which might also be called "lack of belief in God."

Rabbi Mordechai Finley taught that the Jews were not asked to prevail alone against the Giants, they were asked to trust God and to prevail *with God's help*. Rabbi Finley taught, further, that Reform Judaism has long held that religion is based upon acts, and that a belief in faith characterizes the Christian religion and is foreign to Judaism.

Each religion, however, he taught, contains the same elements, taught in different admixtures. One may emphasize, at some point, one element over another, but each contains them all, and it is a mistake to suppose that Judaism does not both recognize and *demand* that spiritual devotion that might be called faith. Rabbi Nachmann taught that life is a narrow bridge, and the most important thing is not to be afraid.

Continuing fear is usually metamorphosed by the sufferer into some more easily assimilated form. Into self-idolatry, for example—"I am immune, for I possess some inchoate excellence." Lack of belief becomes rejection of belief.

My good friends saw, in themselves, heroes who would have, in that time, championed the right, who would have stood up for the Frank family. They, in a fairly benign fantasy, elected themselves wise and powerful and courageous.

Faced with the same situation today, asked to side with, to understand, at the very least to empathize with, that same group, their people, the Jews, they took the part of ignorance and abandonment and sided with their people's enemies.

The novelist W. C. Heinz was a war correspondent in the European theatre. He landed on D-Day and stayed in the front lines until the end of the War.

He wrote that the correspondent was constantly torn between fear and guilt. He had to get up every morning and *choose* to go into battle.

Meanwhile the young men around him had no choice. They fought to live; the correspondent fought to live with himself.

Clerambault's Syndrome

The conversos of Spain escaped the Inquisition by pretending to embrace Catholicism. They acted, in all outward forms, as Catholics but secretly practiced Judaism in their homes. The new converso, the assimilated Western Jew, in a curious inversion, practices no religion whatever, retaining only his self-identification as a Jew.

How odd. This self-identification offers neither protection nor joy—indeed, quite the opposite. It is observably unpleasant to the individual, usually tempered by "But I'm not observant" or "My parents were . . ." and so on; it is not a proclamation but a confession. As such, it can be seen as a wish, and this is, I think, the true link to the converso: the apostate Jew confesses what to him, as to the Inquisition, is a sin.

Just as with the converso coreligionists, his confession is a step toward acceptance by the wider community. The converso could not live, let alone thrive, in Spain as a Jew; the current apostate makes a clean breast of his genetic error in an unconscious hope of thus being acceptable to the Christian community.

Ignorant of religion (his own and that of those he attempts to placate), he unthinkingly performs an act of submission. In this he is as the victim of de Clerambault's Syndrome.

Here the sufferer, awed by the supposed power of another, is driven to offer sexual submission. For example, the new recruit at Marine boot camp must begin and end every sentence with the word "sir." Should he omit the closing, the drill instructor might say "I need you to put the 'sir' on the end, or else I might suspect you're going to end your sentence, 'and I want to suck your ———.' "

The powerful and famous are familiar with the phenomenon of total strangers, in a crowd, miming sexual submissiveness and availability. These afflicted admirers would, perhaps, be mortified to recognize their behavior—they have, in their awe, been regressed, via the most ancient of neural pathways, to an animal state, self-prostrated before a conqueror.

The Marine recruit, however, is rescued from his terror. His psychosis has been induced by the organization that intends, by that means, to assimilate him. He is being broken down so that he may be rebuilt by and in fealty to his new tribe.

But not the apostate. He will continue in a bearable, if regrettable, state of unconscious submission, not recognizing the symptoms of his misplaced—and for that, all the more pathetic—desire to belong.

Why is this desire repressed?

Because he considers it shameful.

Why does he consider it shameful?

Because he has adopted the view of the anti-Semites—his enemies. He is frightened by the presence of a natural urge, *to belong*, as he, ignorantly, feels its most proximate object as forbidden.★

Separated from the Jews, knowing nothing of Judaism except the slander of its opponents, the apostate would transfer his fealty to those he considers the stronger group. His first motion toward them is the offer of a gift: he accepts their notional superiority—he then endeavors to ape what he considers their practices: he confesses his sin. But the Christians never will accept him, and he has rejected the Jews.

What persists? The habit of confession, which is to say, of

★ Cf. the once, and perhaps still, popular psychoanalytic notion of "homosexual panic." Here the adolescent (which is to say, not fully formed) male is terrified by the gap between his burgeoning sexuality and his ability to cathect it safely. He feels unequal to the task and alone in his inability. He is not only frightened but also ashamed. His mind, ever handy, searches for a concrete cause preferable to the terror of the unknown. "What," it reasons, might be the root of this inexplicable shame, which I sense is, somehow, linked to sex?" and the mind grasps (or grasped, in a less-enlightened time) a state conveniently labeled as shameful, "Aha," thinks the adolescent, "I see. I am, unfortunately, turning into a homosexual." We will note that this homosexual panic has nothing whatever to do with homosexuality, nor with the sufferer's actual sexual orientation. It is a neurotic disturbance, borne of ignorance and needless shame and is congruent, mechanically, to Jewish self-loathing.

anomie, which is his ongoing state; it has become a constant of his own self-image, indeed an article of unreasoning, fervent belief.

He has in effect created a new, unnamed religion. It does not offer peace, but it has the merit of familiarity.

Moses and Monarchy

The wicked son is, largely, a phenomenon of twentieth-century America. He shares with his country the delusion that a vague notion of his own benevolence will protect him in the world. In what this benevolence consists is unclear. It is somehow allied to the idea of inherited merit: that one's father fought in World War II, the American feels, will somehow win from the descendants of other nations good wishes, understanding and, truth be told, submission.

But gratitude, as Eric Hoffer tells us, is a greatly overrated sentiment and never to be relied upon.

Why should heredity confer impugnity? A moment's reflection teaches that it will not.

Further, the fallen-away Jew is bifurcated in his magical understanding of inheritance: he has been freed to espouse or enjoy a doctrine of lassitude and privilege by the same fathers whose religion and race he discards. "I am Jewish but not *too* Jewish" can be understood as a statement of secularity and ingratitude, to wit: because my ancestors suffered persecution and *prevailed*, I will renounce their struggle and call my ingratitude enlightenment; my ignorant scorn of the Israelis and their struggle will be called championship of the oppressed, my ignorance of religion common sense; and my supercilious superiority to its practices a licensed diversion.

Licensed by whom or what? This scoffing at the seder table, the proud announcement of X decades without having set foot in a synagogue, the delighted self-mockery at wearing a handout *kippah* at a wedding? This boorish, ignorant behavior, unthinkable in practice toward the customs of another, are practiced against his own kind—good clean fun to the wicked son.

I attended a bar mitzvah, proudly announced by the parents as the first in their family in sixty years. The reception was lavish; vast jumbo shrimp were the first course, and an African band serenaded the large group. The bar mitzvah's uncles came onstage to congratulate him, one of them stark naked and covered only by the fronds he had filched from the stage's décor. He delivered his congratulations in a "darky" voice, to some merriment from the group.

Those left at the foot of the mountain waited for Moses to bring down the law. They overcame their fear with ceremony—they melted down the gold they had taken from Egypt, formed it into a bull calf, and worshipped it. They, again, were not unaware but rather *too* aware of the closeness of God, and they felt shame—such shame that it reduced them to buffoonery, to idolatry, to a depraved attempt to escape from the knowledge of their own unworthiness.★

What is this supposed store of cost-free merit upon which the fallen-away Jew relies? It is Mama's Bank Account. There is nothing there.

His historic impugnity (call it fortuitous or God given) has created arrogance. The arrogance will vanish, however, in time of trouble, for in the pogrom the apikoros will look for a house with a mezuzah, and the afflicted will plead to be taught to pray.

This should be evident to even the most comfortable. But the reason of the apikoros has been troubled. Like the American electorate, he has been deranged by freedom of choice.

We humans autonomically endow a leader with magical powers. It is a tropism allied to that of love, wherein, we are reminded, lovers cannot see the petty follies they themselves commit.

The chemical, neurological endowment of the leader induces a sort of madness as the masses are now unable to impute to the leader humanity. His supporters think him incapable of human frailty, his detractors see in him nothing else. He has been raised to supernatural status.

Our human tendency toward self-aggrandizement and

★ A close friend of many years was in the hospital, near death. The priest came by on his daily rounds, inquired after my friend and asked if he would like to take communion that day. My friend said, "Father, I don't deserve it." "No one does," the priest said.

our sad knowledge of our own worthlessness are cathected onto the elected leader; for good or ill, he is no longer human. The will to believe in the leader is so strong that even elected governments devolve inexorably toward monarchy—consider, for example, the Roosevelts, the Kennedys, Gore, Bush, the Sinatras.

In a democracy, however, the electorate is unaware of the process, and the residual illusion of *rational choice* blinds the voter not only to his wish for monarchy but also to its essential nature, which is acknowledgment that the role of the monarchy's leader is *symbolic*.

In the actual, contemporary monarchy, that is evident which in its supposedly democratic imitators is hidden: that the individual, and that a society must govern itself, as the monarch is a figurehead.

Acknowledgment of the nonpotent nature of this figurehead *diffuses* the unconscious, unavowable, infantalizing wish to be ruled; after which the individual now-aware voter can get down to the business at hand: the unromantic, mundane, and most necessary day-to-day government of and by fallible human beings—the schools, the sewers, the crumbling bridges, and the price of corn.

Aware of the longing for monarchy, the conscious member of modern democracy is free to dispute, to embrace or reject, pronouncements of government without feelings either of self-aggrandizement or treason. The assimilated Jew does not realize that he is in a similar position. He is involved in a *monarchial* proposition: Moses has been interposed between him and God, to rid him of shame, to allow him to diffuse the terror of the Almighty. In so doing, he is not only required but free to participate in the life of his people.

The Chumash is the story of the rebellion against the Divine. Moses dies, but the Jewish people has not yet resolved its problem. Here we are like the unfortunate family, enmeshed in an ongoing, communal neurosis. The supposed authority figure (Moses, the parent), the person understood as cause or arbiter of this trauma, dies—the trauma, however, continues. As we see today, where the naked uncle in the palm frond, the Jewish champion of the PLO, the proudly ignorant Jew reenacts, daily, compulsively, interminably, the Korah Rebellion, the sin of the golden calf, the sin of the spies.

This person, in the shame of his own self-knowledge, in the shame of his knowledge of his own self-sufficiency, must and will create false gods, as does the electorate. Only the recognition of the actual sovereignty of Another will set him free to reason.

Neurotics

What is it that drives some intellectuals in free countries to hate their native land and wish for its annihilation? In a Western democracy the adversary intellectual is not only against his country . . . but he sides with animals against man, with the wilderness against the sown. Predictably, an adversary intellectual who is a Jew sides with the Arabs against Israel. . . .

One who hates what most people love probably savors his own uniqueness. The adversary intellectual cannot actually wreck a society, and he cannot seize power, but by discrediting and besmirching a society he undermines the faith of its potential defenders.

—ERIC HOFFER, *In Our Time*

My friend the bookseller had just come from what in previous times would have been known as a roadhouse. The roadhouse was on a two-lane blacktop in northern New Hampshire, and frequented by a rather hard-drinking crowd.

There my friend ran into an unfortunate fixture of the neighborhood, a logger who had, among other things, been convicted some years earlier of manslaughter. He was now returned to the community a murderer and a confirmed wife beater and drunk.

"He bought me a drink," said my friend the bookseller, "and I was so proud."

On the one hand, my friend is and had been an absolute mainstay of the community for over forty years. He and his wife had raised two boys and put them through college. The entire family worked at the bookshop year-round and was involved in every aspect of the community.

Why was the bookseller proud to be drinking with a thug and a felon?

Because the bookseller was a Jew.

I would call this pride self-loathing, but Mr. Hoffer suggests that it is self-aggrandizement. I believe both understandings are correct.

The bookseller had, for years, been the main mover in a free-form, yearly community celebration that was called a "seder." It was not, however, a celebration of the Exodus from Egypt nor a feast of matzah. It was, year to year, an expression of enlightened liberal sentiment (usually outrage) on the issue of the day. That issue was, again as per Mr. Hoffer, always some enormity perpetrated either by the

U.S. government or by the State of Israel. My friend, additionally, wrote a column for the local paper in which he frequently took the side of the Palestinians.

Karen Horney wrote of neurotics that one must take into account their real, and understandable, pride—that they have each crafted a strategy for getting through the day and that the strategy works. This pride of achievement, she continued, compounds the difficulty of unraveling a neurotic behavior—it is not only that the behavior works *faute de mieux*, but that it offers the practitioner a true sense of accomplishment.

Perhaps this is the meaning of "pride" as applied by the bookseller to his relationship with the wife beater and murderer. Perhaps he was taking pride not in that he, a vile Jew, had been singled out for friendship, but that his grand scheme allowed him to deal with an unorthodox social situation by simple interjection of his incipient anti-Semitism— that he had crafted a tool so good that its use could be applied to a multiplicity of problems.

Offered companionship by a true enemy of the community he and his family had worked so hard to serve, he dealt with his unease by recurring to the known and tested: "I am a Jew, and Jews are vile," and found, to his delight, that it served.

In the *Economist* of 5 June 2004, I find the obituary of Roger Straus Jr.: "He was born into oodles of money, to a mother who was a Guggenheim heir, and a father whose family owned Macy's department store. Yet, as he revealed two years ago in an interview in *The New Yorker*, his Jewishness often worked against him. Mr. Straus felt victimized at his Episcopalian private school."

I read this thumbnail history somewhat differently: it was not his "Jewishness" that worked against him, it was the Episcopalian private school; else one might say of a rape victim, "Her femaleness worked against her."

But the remainder of the paragraph has a happier twist: "In later years he proudly called himself 'a New York Jew'; but it had taken time."

Good for you, Mr. Straus, and rest in peace.

I've never understood the idea of the "tough Jew" as anomaly. The only Jews I knew, growing up, were tough— children of the Depression, soldiers or wives of soldiers in World War II, my grandparents' generation, who came here with nothing and built lives for us.

Why would an individual, or populace, the heirs to not one but a hundred generations of dedicated, tough, resourceful Jews, desire to posit and then join an imaginary passive group? For, in my experience, any person or group so identifying itself will *absolutely* attract a raptor.

It is not "the Jews" who are other-than-tough but this or that individual Jew. And it is helpful, indeed, to note Mr. Hoffer's perception, that their harm comes not from outright action, but from the demoralizing influence of their neurosis upon the group.

Such influence *must* be recognized and be resisted.

It is, I believe, unlikely that any self-professed antagonist to Israel, and so to the Jew, can be brought by force of outside reason to recognize and correct this self-serving apostasy—but I think understanding of such *as* self-serving, rather than self-loathing, may aid an observer to a more useful understanding.

The Wicked Son

The costs of assimilation are many. They include fatigue, sorrow, loneliness, and self-doubt.

Ignorance leads the troubled to ascribe their anomie to their heritage rather than to their rejection of it. Their efforts are not unlike the political pronouncements of those who have, through faith, "cured" themselves of homosexuality—if those efforts were, in fact, a sham, and their only reward the knowledge of hypocrisy, they must, of course, be defended all the more vehemently.

In *The Lay of the Last Minstrel*, Walter Scott writes that the nonpatriotic soul "goes back to the dust from whence he sprung, unwept, unhonored, and unsung."

These words, though perhaps problematically applied to the nonpatriotic, are curiously true of the apostate, who would not stand with those who would stand with him.

This is the wickedness of the wicked son. He feels free to enjoy his intellectual heritage, the Jewish love of learning, and reverence for accomplishment; he enjoys, aware or not, a heritage of millennia of Jewish Law and values; he enjoys his very life, which would have been denied him and his ancestors in the Europe they suffered to leave; he enjoys the right to protection from the community he disavows and, through it all, parrots, "My parents were Jews, but I do not consider myself a Jew."

This is certainly wickedness.

Were we to find such behavior in our children, we would weep. I believe we should weep when we discover it in our peers.

There is, of course, a certain commonality or collusion of apostasy, but see the fallen-away Jews, nonobservant, dismissive of their people as a people, opposed to the State of Israel, and yet clubbed up with their like, autonomically formed into that community alone wherein they enjoy life: that of their fellow Jews. Can this be accident? These enclaves of the rational?

For Jews feel most comfortable in the community of Jews. Who can deny it? Freed from either the scorn or the "understanding" of the non-Jewish world, the Jew can be himself. Are six thousand years of cultural and genetic and religious affinities to be abrogated by the brave individual embrace of secularity? Demonstrably not. Examine the elective affinities of the apostate Jew—the communities, the clubs, the professions, the resorts—all the inhabitants are Jews.

But such affinity stops at the temple door—while the assimilated, again, confects prodigies of ad hoc and essentially religious observances and traditions, one of which is the ritual proclamation of secularity. For "I am Jewish, but I do not practice" is as much of a ritual as the Shema. Both are protestations of faith in a superior power—in the first case, assimilation; in the second, God.

But the sad truth is that the world hates a turncoat.

Our American language, indeed, has no value-free term for one who turns against any organization (even the criminal) to which he belongs: turncoat, whistle-blower, stool pigeon, informer. Even the most high-minded and courageous acts performed by a member against an organization malignant to the community in general cannot be characterized free of opprobrium.

Jews may, of course, convert, in complete good faith, to other religions, but that good faith convert, having found and chosen his own path to God, is not likely to identify himself (primarily) in terms of what he has *rejected*. The wicked son must guard himself against fear of a, in fact, inevitable scorn from those to whom he proclaims his freedom from his despised heritage.

What company does he seek out to lessen the threat?

That of his fellow Jews.

Jacob and Esau

Esau was a hunter, while Jacob dwelt in the tents. He wanted to be close to his mother, Rebecca.

She felt that her son could achieve his rightful due only through trickery, and she so schooled him. Jacob was attracted to the family of Laban, his uncle. Laban was a cheat and cheated Jacob of his promised wife, Rachel, and, further, reneged on the bargain of Jacob's rightful wages.

Jacob resorted to trickery to extort his due from Laban and took with it a bit extra, a profit beyond that promised to him, for his trouble—a form of revenge, mischief, or reparations.

Jacob reencountered Esau at Peniel and prepared for war. In the night before the expected battle a man came to Jacob. And Jacob wrestled with the man all night long, until the man smote him on the hip joint, which is to say, the genitals. The man then blessed Jacob but told him that his name would thereafter be changed.

The name "Jacob" derives from the Hebrew word for

"heel"—as, in the Torah, Jacob, at birth, caught Esau's heel in an attempt to deprive him of the benefits of primogeniture.

The lowly, despised Heel is transformed by his combat with the man into the new thing, the new name, the new man, Israel, which means "He will fight with God."

The man of the tents, the heel, the boy tied to his mother, the deceiver (and thus deceived) is given a new struggle. The fact of strife remains, but the struggle is no longer ignominius but noble.

Jacob and Esau are, of course, one. We might say two sides of the same being, or two aspects of human nature, or of the human being caught at the moment of transition from hunter-gatherer to farmer.

Esau-Seir means "red" and is connected to Adam, whose name also means "red" and "earth."

Eric Hoffer writes in *In Our Time*, "The age-old enmity between the warrior and the trader becomes particularly interesting when seen in the light of recent events which indicate a kinship between the two as close as to make possible an interchange of roles. We have seen the German and Japanese warriors become the world's foremost traders, and the Jews the foremost warriors."

And yet. Some Jews seem to delight in a miching and confused attraction-repulsion to power. Are we Jacob, the boy who stayed in the tent, or Esau, the great hunter?

Hoffer writes elsewhere of the, unfortunately, well-recognized phenomenon of the Jewish lover of his enemies—

that Jew who takes staunch pride in supporting, for example, the Palestinian cause. This neurotic behavior he understands as the urge to feel special—not content with being a member of a group and race (or even a *non*member), the so afflicted wish to gain power and status at the expense of the group.

With whom, however, does this deluded soul think to stand? As I drive to synagogue on the Saturday before Easter, I see a church festooned with a banner advertising a film.

The film is *The Passion of the Christ*, and the banner looks to have been manufactured by the film's distributor.

I am filled with awe and envy. How wonderful it would have been to have invested in the film, I think, in the name of my synagogue.

Would not a smarter man have foreseen the film's phenomenal success? How much better for the Jews to profit from than to decry a dramatic treatment which is but another manifestation (along with the *Protocols of the Elders of Zion* and the Final Solution) of that Jew-hatred engendered by the Gospels. For if you cut us, we will most certainly bleed, but weep and one weeps alone.

What a burden, to be of a despised race.

Some have been forced to resort to arms, in Eretz Israel, some to lamentations, some to apostasy, and some, like Jacob, to chicane. (Recall my fantasy of film investment.)

How is one to walk the straight and narrow between a

desire simply to get on with one's life and the fear of cowardice, between Jacob and Esau?

The bookseller will identify with the murderer, in a hidden wish for protection. The more fortunate, braver, or more self-aware will pose the question (which is the struggle with the Man): Who am I? Am I the lowly and despised Heel, or am I that person who will wrestle with God? The question's answer will not bring an end to strife but will recast the battle for identity, offering the combatant the option of struggle with dignity.

Belonging

To me, real life consists in belonging.

I've spent most of my life in show business, and I never have walked through the stage door or onto a movie set without the thrill of belonging. On the stage or set, one is surrounded by like-minded people speaking a common language, having a common goal. This group is not opposed to the world but a world-within-the-world—small, contained, cohesive, mutually responsible.

I never served in the military and regret it. Dr. Johnson wrote that every man thinks more meanly of himself for not having been a soldier. I attest to his observation but have always felt graced in the other hermetic groups to which I have belonged.

What have I found in them? Filial piety, humor, language, a responsibility to learn and to instruct, a sense of timelessness and history: "So-and-so's father was one of the key grips on *Love in the Afternoon*—*his* father worked for D. W. Griffith—do you know what happened on the set *yesterday*?" (this introduction followed by an anecdote which may or may not have happened yesterday and, equally, could have been set— as it was equally likely—on the first day of the silent era).

This vertical and horizontal community creates incredible solidarity. On the shoot, everything is taken away or is about to be taken away: sleep, health, family, comfort— everything except a sense of shared purpose.

Show-business people share a soft pity for those who would like to join but cannot or have not. For we have, in the dream of the ten-year-old child, run away to the circus, and the poor wistful reasonable souls on the outside stayed home.

The Talmud compares the love of the Torah to that of a "wife with a narrow womb"—a fairly graphic description.

Life on the set eschews wealth and position as beside the point. The powerful may, mistakenly and unfortunately, exercise prerogatives, but those actually involved in movie-making understand that such behavior deprives the offender of the chiefest joy of participation, which is immersion in the community.

Knowledge, courtesy, goodwill, stoicism, wit, these moral acts and observances enlighten and spiritualize the set. Each day the involved, which is to say, observant, goes home having learned a lesson. It may be in mechanics; it is, at least as often, in ethics: how to behave in a difficult situation, how to control fear, anger, sloth—indeed, lust or greed. These lessons—in the larger world, difficult—are made salutary by the respect and approval bestowed by the group on their mastery. Small acts of helpfulness, forbearance, or even silence, are powerfully endorsed.

It is, to me, that tribe of which one dreams, which many seek in this or that confected enterprise: sports bar, sports rooting, paintball, "bonding" expeditions. The opposite of this tribal life is a life of anxiety, loneliness, and loss.

Analgesics include consumption, power and the quest for power, envy, grievance, and hatred, as we, in each case, compare ourselves and our state to that of others, and end the comparison either in arrogance or loathing. Or in grief.

This love of belonging, as does the love of the wife with the narrow womb, impels one to service, attention, and consistency. It prompts one to greater understanding. How wonderful to have such an object of devotion.

When I was a child, I played the piano. How good, I thought, to know all one could know about the instrument: how to play it, how to write for it, how to *repair* it, how to *build* it. And some, in life, are lucky to have such a love. One fellow collects pocketknives. He finds romance in collectors' magazines that are mere columns of figures: "Case, folding hunter: 6265/1." Ah, he says.

Gun collectors, stamp collectors, aviation enthusiasts, gardeners, golfers, these know the meaning of zeal. Collectors see each other at a swap meet, looking for that missing piece. And as we search, we are drawn, we are awakened, to other possibilities, vertically, across the spectrum of interests and, horizontally, back through time *and* forward to the similarly devoted. As our collection takes shape, we muse on or plan a completion, a bequeathal, and rejoice at the discovery or induction of an acolyte.

And yet, what is it? The stoics say, "Of what is it made?" The collector's object of love is only a bent piece of steel, a stamp, a scrap of shaped wood, a colored plate. Ah, but, we say, the romance is not even limited to the actual object. Are we not moved to a similar state of bliss by mere contemplation of its *ideal*, its description, model number, recipe?

It is said there are three happy states of the collector: discovery, possession, and dispersal, each of which, during its period of sway, is supreme: to thirst after, to enjoy, to share; until the burning desire, in the perfected state, is clear of attachment either to the thing itself or to its contemplation—devotion, over time, having been blessed with a repletion of gratitude, sufficient unto itself.

And yet. This love of community, this love of knowledge, this joy of immersion in history, this thirst for group approval, for moral perfection, this endless variety of vertical and horizontal connection, these are all open to the Jew, both his right and his responsibility, and Judaism goes begging.

Chesed/Gevurah

I knew a fellow who prided himself on the view that perhaps O. J. Simpson did not kill his wife.

A laudable disposition to open-mindedness decayed, in late twentieth century, in America, into an inability to arrive at conclusions. Much of what has come to be muddle-headedness derives from a lack of stake in any outcome. The forces operating on our lives seem increasingly remote, less understandable, and so have become *moot*—capable of being discussed but incapable of being understood, let alone affected.

But there are issues upon which one must take a stand. One of them, I believe, is that of Jewish identity; for not to do so is to remove oneself from the group.

An editorial in the *Washington Times* referred to George Soros as someone who "somehow managed to survive the Holocaust" (quoted in an editorial in *The New York Times*—read it again—it is an accusation).

But the wicked son feels he may, with impugnity, abstain when the roll is called.

George Stevens, the great American film director, was with his Army unit at the liberation of Dachau. He returned, some eight years later, with his son, who photographed him. In the photograph he is dressed in civilian clothes, wearing a raincoat, in back of his *Duschbad*—shower bath. His face is, to me, the face of responsibility.

It is not that one might, through laziness, fatigue, or lack of courage, shrink from responsibility, that one might be untrue to the sufferings of one's fellow Jews—one cannot possibly be other than untrue, one *must* falter; but one must try again to regard and to assess the unimaginable: that there are, have been, and, sadly, will be, those who wish one and one's kind dead because of one's heritage, race, or religious beliefs.

Self-exclusion *must* arise from a feeling of indemnity. Converted Jews were hounded by the Inquisition well into the nineteenth century—the reluctant convert and the true convert both liable to accusations of "a lack of sincerity," and killed. As were the German-Jewish despisers of the *Ostjuden* (the Polish Jews), those comfortable, assimilated Jews who imagined that anti-Semitism was not a psychosis on the part of the majority populace, but rather that group's correct understanding of the "Jewish plague" that endangered them all.

But all who stayed went to the ovens.

For the Jew to say, of the Jew-haters, I agree with them; and to say, I do not have facts to judge, but, perhaps some of what they say is true, misses the point. The point is that, to the jihadist, to the anti-Semite, the shtetl Jews and the German banker, the West Bank settler and the Ohio dentist are *one*. To suggest that the rational thinker is exempted, either through identification with the aims of killers, or through a laudable withholding of judgment, posits a position of impugnity. This feeling of impugnity—as the terrorists have limited themselves neither geographically, nor to a degree of consanguinity—is madness. To them, as to the editorialist at the *Washington Times*, a Jew is a Jew.

The acquiescent apikoros basks in sloth. This person is not righteous but cowardly, and neither sloth nor cowardice will protect him if, God forbid, the hammer of the Crusades, the Inquisition, the Holocaust, the jihad falls toward him. Who will protect him? His fellow Jews.

What Israel Means to Me

Noam Chomsky was interviewed in *Heeb* magazine, July 2004:

Q. What about recent incidents in Europe and the Arab world. It would seem to involve pretty acrobatic leaps of logic to say that those are not anti-Semitic.

CHOMSKY: In Europe there's a large Muslim population, and much of it has been driven to fundamentalist Islam. They display hatred toward Jews that is a reflection of Israeli practices. I mean, if you carry out a brutal and vicious military occupation for 35 years . . . it has consequences. Sometimes the consequences can be quite ugly, and, among them, is the burning of synagogues in France. Yes, it's anti-Semitism, but Israel insists on it. Remember, Israel does not call itself the state of its citizens. The high court in Israel declared over 40 years ago that Israel is the sovereign state of the Jewish People, in Israel and the Diaspora.

In effect, since the Jewish State has proclaimed itself as the home of all Jews within its borders and in the diaspora, for the diaspora Jews to do other than renounce this, as a usurpation of their personal rights to self-determination, of their rights as undifferentiated citizens, is tantamount to their endorsement of that which Mr. Chomsky sees as a criminal enterprise (the State of Israel).

Mr. Chomsky, a Jew, does not recognize the Jewish State's right to existence; he *does*, however, recognize as somehow morally binding the pronouncements of this phantom state. Upon whom are they binding? Upon members of that state's predominant religious group wherever they may live.

These diaspora Jews, we will note, reside in countries whose right to existence, presumably, Mr. Chomsky *does* recognize. For example, France. France, as a sovereign nation, then, has the right, as Israel does not, to protect its citizens. The right, however, does not, in Mr. Chomsky's view, extend to French Jews—their right to live unmolested and in peace has, alone among French citizens, been somehow abrogated by the actions of another state.

Various Muslim countries, including Syria and the Palestinians have, as a matter of both religious and political doctrine, repeatedly expressed their intention to destroy the Israeli Jews. This intent is not an adjunct of a territorial dispute but an essential component of their polity—this hatred cannot be mitigated by concession, by negotiation, even by capitulation; it can only be assuaged through blood.

Mr. Chomsky does not seem to object to this incitement to genocide; neither does he extend the same standard for extraterritorial guilt to diaspora Muslims.

The United States, in the aftermath of September 11, has taken care (it may be insufficient, but it is a matter of national policy) to protect the rights of Arab-Americans— on guard lest an ignorant and frightened populace turn on the guiltless because of their mere ties of race or religion to criminals.

This would seem to be a most basic operation of human justice—for to endorse a vendetta against the innocent based on race or religion is here seen, and simply seen, as obscene criminality. Mr. Chomsky, however, sees fit to understand and applaud such actions, as long as they are carried out against the Jews.

This is anti-Semitism—it is race hatred and incitement to murder.

That Mr. Chomsky wears the mantle of respect, that he occupies the position of "intellectual," and that he continues to confuse and debauch the young with his filth is a shame. To abide this shame is part of the price of living in a free society.

Israel is a free society. The rights of the minority, of the oppressed, indeed, of the criminally foolish are protected. Mr. Chomsky would be as free in Israel to pronounce this nonsense as he is in the United States. Were he to find himself in the Arab World, he would be persecuted as a Jew (as, indeed, he might in France). And were he, God forbid, persecuted, Israel would offer him a home, under the Right of Return.

That is what Israel means to me.

Well Poisoning

There have always been unstated but universally under-stood exemptions in the laws governing human behavior. In this country the poor are permitted adultery and a certain degree of spousal abuse and internecine murder but are barred from theft; the rich are allowed to steal and to take drugs but are punished for sexual misconduct and physical crime.

Similarly, on the world stage, Moslem extremists may not bomb New York, but rational human beings—some, to their shame, Jews—hold that Jihadists may bomb Jerusalem. The apologists are or pretend to be incapable of differentiat-ing between the lamentable and decried death of civilians in a military reprisal, and the targeted strategic murder of schoolchildren.

This license is precarious, for the Palestinians, raised by unsettled Western thought to superhuman status, enjoy that status only as a counterpoise to the bestiality of the Jews. Should the Palestinians choose, in their uncontrollable sorrow and extremity, to bomb New York, they would find their license revoked.

The midrash has it that the Egyptian taskmaster whom Moses killed had spent the previous night raping the wife of the Jewish man who was now being whipped. When the man came to work that morning, the taskmaster singled him out as a fit object of scorn and abuse—a man who would not even stand up for his wife.

And, indeed, the man submitted to this further brutality, and none of the Jews spoke up; finally, Moses could take no more. He stepped in and struck the taskmaster down. The Jews would not defend their fellow, for they had both the status and the mentality of slaves; and this, perhaps, may be seen as Moses' first exposure to the problem of Jewish passivity, the problem that would plague him through his life and persists to our own day—that some may identify with their oppressors—the slave with their strength, the apostate Jew with their reason.

Hooked-Nose Jews, or
Let's Make It Pretty

But, Lord! to see the disorder, laughing, sporting, and no attention, but confusion in all their
service, more like brutes than people knowing the
true God, would make a man forswear ever seeing
them more and indeed I never did see so much, or
could have imagined there had been any religion in
the whole world so absurdly performed as this.

—SAMUEL PEPYS, *Diary*, October 14, 1663

Many of the country's synagogues are defaced, not by
anti-Semites but by their own members.

I was taught by Rabbi Larry Kushner that a display of
name plaques, degrees of contribution, and the like, that
identification of congregation members by what and how
much they had contributed, is a religious offense. And I
believe it. His attitude is, in fact, so vehement that trans-

gression is understood not merely as an offense but an obscenity. But, some congregation members ask, how will we raise money otherwise—it has always been done this way (one of the Three Cardinal Arguments, the other two being: it's a slippery slope; and, you know and *I* know, but unless we win the support of the ignorant, we cannot implement our intelligent plans).

Rabbi Kushner, nonetheless, throve at his beautiful shul for twenty-seven years—a shul in which there were no name plaques, which published no levels of donation, which took real pride in the inviolability of the rabbi's rule.

What did this mean? That people were respected for their learning, for their ability to sing trope, for their service to the Congregation, for their more generalized ethical accomplishments: their forbearance or humor in difficult situations, for their ability to lead or follow. The simple rule, in short, inculcated a host of virtues. For what do these plaques mean, other than: so-and-so (the donor) is better than you or I?

They can have no other meaning. They are the worship of wealth in the spot most inauspicious for that devotion. We Jews are instructed *not* to display any representation of the human form. How much more objectionable to display a representation of man reduced to an invidious cipher.

One may, in this display, see a reversion to priestly Judaism. The tensions between the priests and the rabbis at the turn of the Common Era is commemorated, among our Christian neighbors, by the story of Jesus. Jesus, a rabbi, came into the Temple to cleanse it of practices he found in contravention of Jewish Law (the task, then as now, of *every* rabbi).

Many depictions of Jesus, including *The Passion of the Christ*, show him as a rather Aryan-looking (that is, non-stereotypically Jewish) fellow, surrounded, in most cases, by his hook-nosed opponents, the Jews.

The Christians have no prohibition against the depiction of the human form, indeed, of their gods; and one may see, in this case of the Vulgate rendition (the film), the possibility of great error. For if Jesus is shown as of another race than that of his brothers, might that not facilitate (as it certainly has done) race hatred, anti-Semitism, and an interpretation of certain objectionable parts of the Gospel to the detriment of common sense and, indeed, of their essential message?

Rabbi Kushner and his shul also composed the first egalitarian siddur in the Reform Movement (V'taher Libenu, 1980). In it God is referred to, not as He, but, simply, as God.

As with the prohibition on nameplates, this originally disruptive restriction forced the worshipper to constantly confront the true and deeper meaning(s) of the restriction: God, one thought fifty or a hundred times during the liturgy, is not "He." God is not "She," God is not human, and I am incapable of the formulation of God's nature. God is a mystery.

If, to the Jews, God is not a mystery, then what is God?

Perhaps God is a fungible commodity, and the more one

spends, the greater share one has in God. How wise, then, of the tradition, to put certain things beyond our human reach, to control various aspects of eating, sex, dress, speech—of, in short, our daily lives. For the notion that all prohibitions are subject to reason, interpretation, and convenience turns organized religion into an empty experience of self-help, which is to say, of "self."

Why do some Jews reject their religion and their race? For two reasons: because it is "too Jewish" and because it is not Jewish enough.

The true reason may not be clear to the apostate, and he or she may in fact confuse one end of the spectrum with the other. Surrender is frightening, and surrender to one's own tradition, race, and heritage is, demonstrably, the most frightening of all. Witness the hordes of Buddhists, ethical culturists, agnostics, practitioners of yoga, Jews for Jesus, etc., these hordes composed almost entirely of disaffected Jews.

To these, as to the anti-Semites full stop, there is something (find a mark on the spectrum from nonfulfilling to obscene) about the oldest, wisest, and most persecuted yet longest enduring religion in the history of the world. To these the ethical, physical, and spiritual achievements of our race are as nothing; the fact of Jews' accomplishments, vastly out of proportion to our representation in the population is, in itself, a matter of confusion and often of obloquy.

Many of these fallen-away consider their race, and, necessarily (though not necessarily overtly or consciously) themselves, an object of scorn. These Jews act in ignorance, and, truth be told, perhaps in cowardice, positing a "general culture," somehow possessing, magically, more beauty, wisdom, tolerance, or "acceptability" than their own.

This is an urge to overcome some basic shame; but, as Freud told us, the resistance *is* the neurosis—and the supposed cause of shame does not exist. All that exists is the repressive mechanism.

This device shifts shape, operating sometimes in the guise of "common sense," sometimes as "cleanliness." It is said it is common sense that people will give more to a synagogue that blandishes their names and proclaims their generosity. Well, it may be common sense, but it is not Judaism.

The urge to elaborate, to rationalize, to bypass the unconscious and bring "pure reason" to bear, is the death of both art and religion. They exist to bring us closer to a mystery. "Rational" Judaism supplants spirituality as the cautionary tale supplants the bedtime story, substituting instruction in the obvious for awe.

The constant battle against personification and rationalization, against our all-too-human desire to cast ourselves as God, is not a prerequisite for the practice of religion; it *is* the practice of religion. The ignorant Jew may feel a certain queasiness at involvement in a process that requires him to submit to something greater than himself. The reluctance is human. To characterize it as rational abhorrence of Judaism is self-contempt.

The High School Car Wash

What would Margaret Mead make of our high school car wash? This most American, least offensive outpouring of hijinks, this enlistment of good clean fun in the aid of the band or the debating club is, of course, a wet T-shirt contest featuring jailbait.

Imagine a Web site full of these nubile and forbidden young women minimally clothed and dripping wet; logging on might open the computer operator to charges of trafficking in pornography. But there, in the high school parking lot, he can ogle the girls to his heart's content, and get his van washed, too.

Why is this permitted? It is permitted because the true nature of the entertainment is as hidden to the participant as it is to his potential detractors.

So it is with anti-Semitism. Many who enjoy the benefits of hatred as a harmless entertainment would be shamed to have their hidden vice brought to public view. Unfortunately, they run little risk, as the vice is both communally

shared (as at the car wash) and, *were* it brought to consciousness, deniable under various heads.

These headings include (a) I am merely speaking against
Israel, I have nothing against the Jews per se; (b) I am merely
stating the obvious, I mean no harm to individual Jews or to
the Jewish people, but it is a fact that Jews control (*fill in this
space*)—I do not say this is good or bad, only that it is so; and
(c) the Jews killed Christ; I do not say this should influence
our contemporary thinking, but there it is, in the Gospels.

Now, this is all bad enough from a Gentile, but how much
worse when found in the mouth of a Jew.

A joke from a coreligionist:

Q: Why are Jews like manure?
A: A few make things green; too many make everything
stink.

I found this joke significant in that the prospective turncoat was trolling for endorsement using very old bait indeed.
This joke could have been told at the country club in the
1950s (and probably was).

His attempt was pathetic in that he had a tin ear—
contemporary anti-Semitism has largely freed itself of the
possibility of riposte; it has morphed, as has the pedophilic
wet T-shirt contest, into the rhetoric of reason.

Rather than attempting to receive chuckles from the im-
biber of the Rob Roy, the Jew-hater of today may gear his
presentation toward sad nods of the head. Human society,

ever adaptable, has found a way, as usual, around the proscription.

The quiddity of the self-loathing Jew, the opted-out Jew, is his grotesquerie. Both to his people and to the enemies of his people, he is out of step, out of tune, and pathetic—his efforts at assimilation foiling the possibility of contentment with a group to which he actually *belongs*.

Who is this Vedantist, freethinker, newly convinced Episcopalian, detractor of Israel, and whose approval is he courting? Does he think that his brave assertion of his racial taint, coupled with a repudiation of his people's history, traditions, and religion, is going to win him friends anywhere?

It is axiomatic that all military loathe spies and turncoats; is a disaffection fostered by fear of death less worthy of scorn than one fostered by fear of censure?

Who are these poor Jews who think their people stink? And is not the first part of the formulation equally telling, that a *few* Jews make things grow?

Who as per the humorist, are these few? The Jude Suss, the Capo, the House Jew, the Clown, the Danny Kaye "citizen of the world," perhaps the humorist himself, willing to sell out his people to be among the permitted few. Disgraceful.

Philip Roth explored the subject magnificently in *The Human Stain*. Here we see a Jewish professor, hounded from his position for an innocuous offhand comment misunderstood as a racial slur.

We discover, through the book, that the professor is, though, not Jewish at all but an African-American who has spent his whole life passing for white. The misunderstood slur was reported by two African-American students who felt slighted. Thus, as the book ascends from drama to tragedy, we see that the hero's own fault has sought him out, he has run to his appointment in Samarra, the world has set upon him, and he cannot turn for solace to the group that he has, ironically, *in fact* harmed by his abandonment.

This unconvinced Jew is like the lecher at the high school car wash—consciousness of his guilt evident in his wonderful effusive bonhomie.

Judaism:
The House That Ruth Built

I've often heard this story from the fallen-away Jew:

Q: Why did you give it up?
A: I had a bad experience with a rabbi.

The tone with which the explanation is regularly uttered indicates its historic reception with coos and exclamations of sympathy.

But if we remove "rabbi" and substitute "doctor," "dentist," "teacher," or "accountant," the folly of the statement is plain, and it may be understood to mean "I realized that it was optional."

Further, the explanation has something of an indictment about it—i.e., "I also realized that it was wrong—the 'bad rabbi' revealed to me the error of my ways. My late and sad wisdom consisted in recognizing that, of course, the entire organization [Judaism] is, and must be, corrupt."

Q: Why did you never marry?

A: I once met an unpleasant woman.

Oh, really?

Here is a congruent statement, from *The Economist*, 21 August 2005, on Ariel Sharon: "He bears some of the blame for triggering the present violence by his provocative eve-of-*intifada* walk on Jerusalem's Temple Mount."

See the disparity between cause and effect: Sharon-took-a-walk-and-so-thousands-must-die. This must reveal the operation of a hidden mechanism—for the disparity between cause and effect is just too great. A cursory dispassionate analysis shows the progression as absurd. As with the remark about the rabbi. The hidden mechanism in both is anti-Semitism: there is something so wrong about these Jews that, as all know, they are capable of *anything*. They exist to create strife. They are, in short, not human. Let us leave *The Economist* and other good-willed publications to the side, and address the apostate.

He is ensnared in a delusion. His delusion is that he is thinking rationally.

His defense is a tautology: I left because rabbis are bad, rabbis are bad because Judaism is bad, I know this because I met a bad rabbi; or an attack: You, my interlocutor, in your persistence are just like that bad rabbi ("you Jews are all like that").

That his lack of rationality indicts his position does not weaken, but strengthens, his resolved self-removal.

For the unspoken, the resistance, *is* the neurosis, and the neurosis is: self-loathing. All the apostate's information eventuates in self-loathing, which, because it is too painful to feel, is directed outward. "I dare not blame This World, I cannot blame myself—I will blame the Jews."

How might this disaffected and unhappy individual be won back? Only by rote. As they say in A.A.: There are two reasons to go to the meetings—because you want to, and because you don't want to. And, further, "Keep coming back—it works."

The apostate will not be convinced by argument, for his reluctance does not rest on reason.

Just as the writers of *The Economist* could not be swayed by fact: the PLO announced *months* before Sharon's walk that they were stockpiling weapons for terror attacks; Sharon's walk transgressed *no* holy Moslem sites, nor did it, in any way, offend Moslem law or custom; nor by logic: an examination of the phrase "his provocative eve-of-*intifada* walk" reveals a (rather egregious) *post hoc ergo propter hoc* fallacy— *The Economist* states that the walk was provocative because it occurred *on the eve of the intifada.* But to refer to the time of his walk as the eve of the intifada, rather than to refer to the outbreak of violence as the result of the walk, reveals a (conscious or unconscious) understanding by the writer that the intifada was planned *before* the walk. If it were not, the intifada could not have an "eve."

Anti-Semitism is a vile sickness of the mind. It masquerades as reason, and, as any tyranny, *it can never be seen to lose*; for the slightest application of reason to it, as to Nazism, white supremacy, Communism, etc., reveals its total absurdity.

The drink seems, to the alcoholic, the rational, indeed, essential, tool to aid his problematic struggles toward sobriety. And the apostate who once found the "bad rabbi" is similarly challenged not to run, cursing, from his occasional encounters with his religion.

I've seen it, and, perhaps, you have too—the self-proclaimed ex-Jew, scoffing at the funeral, the wedding, the seder, and leaving in dudgeon when his behavior was not tolerated.

What prompts this otherwise rational being to infantile rage? The impossibility of escape.

If his corrupted reason is (by the necessity of basic good manners) silenced, if he is denied sophistry, and *simply forced to sit* in the presence of Judaism, this otherwise civilized being may be driven mad. Many of you have seen it.

Imagine this man at a Japanese tea ceremony, at a Zen Buddhist silent meditation, indeed, at a Catholic mass, a Hopi rain dance. At which would he not sit, if not interested, at the very least, polite? And would he not, if he became bored, turn his attention to whatever good or interest the ceremony might have to offer him?

Would this individual huff and puff and offend those involved in their religious observance? He would rather die. And yet he is driven, *driven*, to decry, to disrupt, and to denigrate the observance of his own people—about which he is as ignorant as he is of the rain dance and to which he owes, as a civilized being, at least as much respect.

What can be done for this person?

Nothing outside of the synagogue.

For, like the alcoholic, *he has got to show up.* The root of self-loathing is so deep, and the necessity for protection from self-knowledge so strong that only enforced participation can begin to overcome what is, finally, a revulsion.

What can reason aid? This person, in ignorance, has chosen his own wisdom over that of millennia, has chosen to turn his back on the people who will, in times of trouble, accept and protect him, has renounced the beautiful observances of his ancestors. He is the gay Republican, an African-American secessionist—his delusion freezes his development, which now must coalesce around apology and denial.

Simple submission would bring him self-knowledge and belonging.

But he must show up.

Here exogamy may come to his aid. The non-Jewish spouse may, in her love, correct his error. Untainted by the folly of self-loathing, never having *met* the bad rabbi, the non-Jew may bring reason to the equation, investigate the spouse's religion and heritage, and bring him or her and the children, little by little, back into the fold.

This is a beautiful and common story—love overcoming hate. It is the love of Ruth: "Wither thou goest, I will go, and your people shall be my people and your God shall be my God." It can move mountains. And it can lead the apikoros back to shul.

Now what happens in shul?

It depends, of course, to a large extent, upon the shul.

The ancient joke has the Jewish castaway found, on the desert island he's inhabited for thirty years. "What are those three bamboo structures?" asks the sea captain. "That over there is my house," says the castaway, "and that over there is my shul." "And what's the third one?" the captain asks. "That," says the Jew, "is the shul I wouldn't be caught dead in."

There is, of course, a real joy in having the shul in which one wouldn't be caught dead. This is known as the joy of belonging, of finding one's like and supporting them. This is a healthy aspect of Judaism—find the rabbi who speaks to you, and worship there.

The newly minted *ba'al teshuva*, of course, may be skittish. Much of the beauty, let alone the good, of the service, and of religion in general, will be revealed only through time. He must make the investment, make a choice, and let *reason* keep him in his seat for those few hours a week.

He will not see a white light and be convinced of the probity of his choice—this would be simply another manifestation of his self-worship, of his apartness—but he may, with safety, think "What would I be doing otherwise? I would be home napping or watching golf on television.

"What can it hurt me to stay here? I am bored? So

I am bored. I've been bored before. See how strong my will is."

And that simple pride in the will may be more than sufficient to fix his attention long enough to create a new habit.

For his self-loathing can and will not be overcome by revelation, it is too ingrained. Only habit will suffice.

The returnee must sit and watch and listen, and, should he do so, eventually he will receive this or that clue.

One clue may be that the Torah contains some material relevant not only to life, and not only to *his* life, but to his very situation: the individual reluctant to acknowledge God, or the Mosaic Law.

Further observation may teach him that, in fact, the *entire* Torah is a commentary on his situation. Having recognized that, he may desire to learn the actual language of the Torah, and, little by little, he will find that the habit of investigation, of study, of curiosity, has supplanted what he will now be able to recognize was the *habit* of apostasy.

Jewish, but Not Too Jewish

How often have we heard or seen Jewish observance treated with scorn: "I'm Jewish, but I'm not observant"; "You go to *Shul*?"; "You support the State of *Israel*?"

How often can one see ignorance of the nature and meaning of language, of symbols and observances, the mezuzah, Shabbos, the holidays, the tallis, payot, Yiddish or Hebrew words or tag lines, without suspecting the ignorant Jew of purposeful obtuseness?

It would be difficult to imagine a Jew living in a Buddhist culture without at least exercising that minute level of curiosity sufficient to distinguish politeness from opprobrium. Jews, however, may live with or near the varying observances or survivals of a culture uniquely their own, and *purposefully* know and wish to know nothing of it.

They may assign this intractability to a simple lack of interest, but such, coupled with a lack of courtesy, must suggest a deeper, less conscious motive. That motive is fear.

Every potential increase in intimacy prompts a retreat from intimacy. The newly married couple fights viciously, and the young wife, proverbially, "runs home to mother." The dating man or woman, dizzy in love, finds, magically, some previously unsuspected and heinous aspect of the beloved's character; the novice is struck with doubts; the cleric undergoes a crisis of faith; all these retreats happen at predictable intervals. They are occasioned not by some new perception but by the prospect of increased intimacy. The Israelites at the foot of Mount Sinai turned their back on Moses not *in spite* of the imminence of God but because of it.

And the apostate or assimilated Jew, who might express delight and wonder at the Japanese tea ceremony and retain these impressions throughout a lifetime, is hard pressed to remember if Rosh Hashanah precedes or follows Yom Kippur. This is not a "lack of interest." It is panic.

Many contemporary rabbis have written most positively about the benefits of Jewish intermarriage. It is not, they point out, non-Jews who dilute and threaten the community, but fallen-away Jews. We have seen frequent examples of the non-Jewish partner bringing his or her spouse back to Judaism.

The primary, striking, and provocative aspect of the non-Jewish spouse's curiosity is the *absence of shame*. Consider the apostate's spoken or unspoken question "Why would you want to do/know *that*?" directed toward a loving spouse. Such a question is rightly understood as horrific, and revelatory of a deep disturbance.

Bravo, then, to the non-Jewish partners, the Jews by choice, the proud Jew, and the otherwise free from apostasy. For they might offer to the rest of us, questioning, confused, ashamed, or remorseful, an answer to the question we have not asked: "Why do I hate my culture?"

Tribal Life

We human beings are happiest in mutual devotion. Even in the shared understanding of the heavy drinker, or the cigarette smoker, there is a degree of love, of mutual service to something greater than oneself. Even in addiction. We see it in the military; we are told that the love of David and Jonathan surpassed even the love of women.

We see this love in those who are blessed in having a life of service. I've spent my life in show business and, in moments of professional trauma, desperation, and temptation, have been chastened and comforted and directed by remembering that it is a calling and that dedication to the ideal is always the answer to the problem of the individual.

In the theatre, in medicine, in law, in public service, we are offered filial piety, honor, tradition, language, a sense of responsibility to instruct, and, so, a sense of timelessness.

Some of us understand that we, in professional lives, in avocations, are shown a tribe and that it is our own tribe. When working with the tribe on the movie set, in the emergency room, indeed, at the sporting event, at the school event, at the amateur theatrical, the military reunion, the collectors' convention, day-to-day considerations are put aside; in the bosom of the tribe, sleep, health, family, comfort can be taken away unnoticed in the joy of belonging.

If questioned, we, meeting in the cold church basement, freezing, sleepless out on the set, drilling with the National Guard, mock the notion of discomfort, our very complaints part of the joy of belonging, and pity those not of the group.

These groups, this tribal life, creates character organically. As we see and admire the individual we wish to please, and to earn his or her respect, through excellence at the group's appointed task, through excellence at courtesy, in reliability, in knowledge. Turn to Sue, Sue will know the answer; Bobby will always be there with a joke when everything goes bust; trust Sam to reduce the complex problem through an anecdote. And we strive to be the equal of these admired individuals in what can only be described as good deeds.

And everyday we learn something. Ah, we say, I now know how to better hold my tongue—I saw Rachel do it.

And those of us in that tribe look out at those who will not join and see the beggars at the feast. It is the tribe of which we dream. You dream of it, too. How do I know?

Virtually every television show is a fantasy of tribal life— the cops, the crooks, the doctors, lawyers, firemen, crime scene investigators; our longing is so strong that for the merest glimpse of its representation, we will sit through the commercials and consider every worthless product in the world. The opposite of life in this tribe is a life of anxiety, lovelessness, and loss.

There are, of course, analgesics. They include consumption, envy, grievance, hatred, as we, in each case, compare ourselves to those who surround us, who we understand to be our adversaries; as we compare ourselves to our neighbors, fellow contestants in a zero-sum endeavor. As we compare ourselves to them, or, indeed, to our *notions* of them. For in this absence of community, which of us knows what, or, in fact, who, our neighbors are?

In trading status, the pursuit of status, wealth, and power, for community, we sign on for the burdens of repression. For the lusted-after preferment is revealed the morning after as nothing. The new car is a problematic hunk of junk as soon as we drive it off the lot; we even know the phrase—Drive it around the block and it loses half its value. The new watch keeps no better time than the old watch, and we wonder why we bought it.

If, however, these pursuits are understood as worthless, whatever are we to do? So we *repress* our knowledge of these objects and of the worthlessness of their pursuit, and much of the rancor we feel toward our neighbors, our business associates, hides fear that they (as well as we) might be aware of our loneliness and longing.

We make demands on no one, and no one makes demands on us. Our business dealings are savage in their lack of courtesy, and we console ourselves that it is the way of the world.

Note that we not only applaud but also envy the firefighters and their families at a funeral; the sailing team, exhausted to death at the end of a race; the egghead scientists at a convention, in the next booth, getting drunk and gossiping about the universe.

Our own enclave, the Jews, exists, in truth, in learning, containing wisdom, solace, tradition, and mutual support. In our connection to the Divine, and to the endlessly fascinating mysteries of our own nature, and that of our fellow acolytes, our race and religion persist, suffused by the ideal, the truth, and our history. It is a gift from God—what greater joy than to support it, to devote ourselves to it, and to enjoy it? For it is written that just as it is forbidden to partake of the forbidden, it is forbidden not to partake of the permitted.

The Jew is not only made and instructed but also *commanded* to live in the world and to enjoy those things God has permitted him—among the chiefest joys: that of belonging.

Apikoros

Epicureanism broke out widely in the 1960s, where we, in America, saw a dissolution of the traditional bonds of religion. Young Jews, most notably, discovered that traditional religion, that is, fealty to or observance of one's faith, limited individuals' "freedom." Was there not, we reasoned then, good in all religions and something to be learned from them all? Would it not make more sense, we told each other, to discard the old and create our *own* observances?

Many recall, and many can still, sadly, witness the couple who write their own wedding ceremony, an essential feature of Epicureanism.

What, one may ask, is the problem with this?

Here is the answer: traditionally, a couple getting married were, wisely, compelled to vow to do not only those things they *wished* to do but also those things the tribe, in its wisdom, had concluded, over time, best augured well for the health and continuation of the marriage.

It is all very well and faux poetic for the young to swear to "respect each other's space" and so forth, but these vows were and are soon abrogated—they were understood, after the glow of courtship had worn off—as subjective (which they are—what, finally, does it mean to "respect another's space"? It means nothing, and signifies nothing other than the writer's intoxication with his own state). Did not these vows, probatively, bear the ultimate stamp of subjectivity? Of course they did. They were composed by the utterer and, so, must be liable to his revision.

These epicurean vows carried neither the weight of tradition and reason, nor the compulsive power of poetry.

"Consecrated to me according to the laws of Moses and the Traditions of the Jewish People," a thousands-year-old formula, a beautiful formula, must awaken more awe in the pretender to the marriage state than writers-group, journal-keeping gibberish.

The Jewish families reasoned "Should not a rational person celebrate *both* Christmas and Chanukah?" found and find that reason is an inferior bond to tradition and that, in failing to transmit the tradition of their people *as paramount*, they were teaching their children that it was inferior.

The apikorsim seemed to think that all traditions were beautiful except their own. Chanukah became an adjunct of Christmas, like the deserving poor person asked to Thanksgiving and "treated just like everyone else." Passover became a pretext for discussion of geopolitics in which, shamefully, the State of Israel could be castigated for supposed crimes against "the deserving poor." Jews became Buddhists, Wiccans, cultists of all stripes. Why particularly the Jews? Because they were deracinated.

As with the compulsive dater, the newly freed Jew understood the cause of his anomie not to be his autoemancipation but his *choice of object*. The serial monogamist says, "I owe it to myself to find the perfect mate, as, finally, does the young person whose time I am wasting. If I discover that, after some investigation, she is not completely right for me, would it not be an act of grace to free her, so that she may look elsewhere?"

Such is the reasoning of the apikoros, seeking out community, wisdom, and solace piecemeal—much of it purchased—from a congeries of spiritual and semispiritual, and merchants of hokum. Japanese drum beating, "self-help" groups and cults, etc., offer to the fallen-away Jew the possibility of repletion.

What pleasures do these? Nothing, per se. The problem is with the Jew himself. For, as with serial dating, his problem is not the discovery of the "perfect one"; his problem is that *he is addicted to the pleasures of the search*.

What pleasures do these pillar-to-post investigations offer? They mask pain and guilt—the pain of abandonment and the guilt of desertion.

For the apikoros, finally, *finally*, knows himself to be a Jew. How do we know? Because of the ritual pronouncements: "My parents are Jewish, but I do not consider myself a

Jew"; "I am a Jew but not a *practicing* Jew"; "*Although* I am a Jew, I disapprove of this Sharon."

This is not the healthy speech of a person who changed religions; it is a confession. (It is only logical that, just as some non-Jews opt into Judaism as offering a covenant more suited to them, some Jews opt out. But those who do, in search of a true holy covenant, are unlikely, indeed, first to proclaim, and second to feel, the need to defend their choice.)

The apikoros is not proceeding toward, but running *from*, something; he identifies the menace as Judaism—a religion and a tradition, increasingly, he does not understand. But he is not running from Judaism (what does he *know* of it, and, more important, what, in it, is threatening?). He is running from his feelings of shame and guilt. And he will, of course, never outpace them.

Where is the hope for this conflicted person?

It is in *observance*.

Here again habit, as all religions know, comes to the aid of the afflicted. The apikoros must accept a situation *in which he cannot choose*—for it is choice, this illusion of freedom that has disturbed him.

The good actor, the good director, understands that the lines *must be said exactly as written*. Why? Because this removes, from the actor, the possibility *and so the necessity* of improvisation.

What does this mean?

Speech awakens emotion in the actor. The mere uttering of the written words will involve the actor in the scene.

The actor, involved in the scene, does not have the self-consciousness to differentiate between a dislike for the written words because they are inept and a dislike for them because they awaken in him feelings he would rather keep hidden.

The only way to maintain the *feeling* of this self-control is by a self-removal from the scene, by the adoption of a role as judge rather than participant. It is literally impossible for the actor to alter the lines to suit and to be involved in the progress of the written scene. One may maintain the *illusion* of superiority to the scene but only at the cost of woodenness.

The observant actor reasons thusly: *since* I cannot differentiate between a dislike of the line as written and a dislike of the emotions it creates, I will *say* the line as written and let the chips fall where they may.

This is the beginning of wisdom in this actor. He comes to realize that the well-written play does not need his help, and the badly written play cannot profit *greater* from his help than to enjoy his *unjudgmental* dedication to the text.

Note that the actor was not *forced* to do the play; he accepted the commission of his own free will and was free to decline. The congregant, the worshipper, similarly, has not been forced to accept the rite (marriage, Communion, brit milah, holiday observance), but, having done so, would be wise, *which is to say rewarded*, to devote himself to the rite per se.

In so doing, he or she will be surprised, as is the actor, finding worth and beauty where none could be suspected. He will be surprised to find himself blessed by the removal of that worthless burden he has, once wishfully, named to himself as "my free will."

The Children of
Kings and Queens

We know that our happiest memories are of submersion in the group. The group may be a happy family, coworkers on a political campaign, the sewing circle, the Army platoon, the scout troop—those times we recognize, in retrospect, we were free of self-consciousness, and the habit of invidious comparison, when those around us were not opponents (real or potential) but brothers and sisters. Indeed, for many in the West, these immersions in the group are the model and sole experience of that happy family that, in its nuclear form, has proved to them hypothetical.

What great joy in setting down that tediously constructed, useless armor we call personality. The demanding maintenance of this false, protective self, we must see, if we do the math, has no commensurate benefit. For that we do not need each other, that we do not long for security, that we do not love rootedness and commonality—is a lie. The resistance *is* the neurosis: it is our terror of loneliness that inspires us to construct the wall. But this wall does not protect us from loneliness but from a consciousness of our fear of it. The loneliness persists, supplanted in the conscious mind by anxiety.

What do we fear? That our protection should fail, and we find ourselves faced with the fact of our unbearable longing. This unnamed anxiety inspires us to fill our time. We compulsively attend classes, we "improve" ourselves, we travel, we play sports, we e-mail, we chatter endlessly, and we complain. We inflict upon our children endless activities with the inchoate sense that this franticness will somehow make them happy.

A little observation shows that it makes the children unhappy—schlepping them from this lesson to that, from this managed birthday celebration to that tutorial. All this is nothing other or better than an early indoctrination in a life of anxiety. The lesson we suggest they learn is that the human being is completely perfectible, if only there were enough hours in the day to permit him to take an infinite number of classes.

Self-help, a schedule of fitness, meditation, yoga, sports, college tutoring, and, in fact, college itself are attempts to fill that which we feel is an endless void. What is the void? Ourselves.

Jewish self-loathing and Jewish anti-Semitism are the theoretical aspect of an empty modern life. The mind finds phobia preferable to free-floating anxiety, so it creates or accepts the idea of an enemy. No, one thinks, "(a) I am so lonely. My desire to belong is so great that were I to face it, and find it unslakable, I would die. I will insulate myself against that desire; (b) I will construct a firewall of confected beliefs and practices, e.g., people are fine on their own, they do not require community but *self-protection*. The desire to belong is a fiction of the weak. I am strong, and will make myself stronger, through various mental and physical techniques of self-perfection."

The maintenance of this false self, however, is constant, and draining, thus "(c) I feel a dread, and sense of unease, for as I, as I have determined, am perfectible, and, on the road to complete self-sufficiency, the cause of this unease must be *an Other*." A historically handy choice is the Jew.

As the enlightened Jew is debarred from identifying himself as "Other," he performs another agile mental feat and directs his anger against "the Jews." But he is not free to fully identify the Jews as others unless he can purge "the Jew in himself."

As with any surgery, there is a certain amount of brutality involved. The pain of self-mutilation, however, may (and must) itself be understood as the result of causes external; the pain must be attributed to the group that one is betraying: "The Jew, the Jews, the Jews."

To you, the wicked son, does it seem logical that the creators, receivers, interpreters and protectors of the Bible for millennia, somehow had it wrong?—that the rabbis, mystics, and prophets who lived to give living sense to immemorial memory were somehow deluded? That Christianity, and

Islam, deriving their brief and their wisdom from the Abrahamic text, are in debt to the Jews for nothing? And I ask you if, in your knowledge of the world, it is unheard of for a too-heavy sense of obligation to foment, in the debtor, a sense of injury?

Perhaps that is the position in which you find yourself.

Does your prized individuality make you content? Does your proclamation of your love of "freedom" free you from your fragmented, commercial attempts to find fulfillment?

Perhaps, as with the inability to find a perfect mate, it is not the parade of prospects but your premises that are incorrect. Perhaps the absence of the perfect Other is another manifestation of the sense of loss manifested in Jewish self-loathing. And perhaps rather than decrying the disappointing nature of the Other, one might investigate the sense of loss itself.

Having determined that one's premises are suspect, might one not, as an exercise, adopt their inverse, to see if that should prove more supportable? Let us suppose, then, that (1) we are not alone; (2) community is good; (3) all human beings long for it; (4) this longing is neither shameful nor foolish; (5) it may be removed by devotion to that very group to which one is, by ties historical, racial, or, indeed, of inclination, entitled to membership; (6) the Jews are a noble race and religion, dedicated for nearly six thousand recorded years, to ethical behavior, study, and the desire to understand that unknowable, unnamable mystery that is indicated by the word "god."

Children, and especially unhappy children, fantasize that the adults with whom they live are not their real parents, that their real parents are noble kings and queens who will one day come for them. This fantasy does not cease with childhood, it strengthens. We defend ourselves against the longing this fantasy represents, and turn against that which would, or might, weaken our defense.

The depth of the wicked son's rancor is the depth of his longing. And, curiously, the childhood fantasy, which we as adults so vehemently disclaim, is true.

We are the children of kings and queens, a holy nation and a kingdom of priests. We are the children of a mystery that has not abandoned us and that has come for us; it is both described and contained in the Torah.

GLOSSARY

afikomen—The final piece of matzah eaten at the Passover seder, the afikomen is broken from a whole piece of matzah early in the seder and put aside for later use. Because the seder cannot be completed until the afikomen is consumed, it has become traditional for children to take the afikomen from the adult leading the seder and ransom it for a gift.

Akedah—The story of the binding of Isaac, which appears in Genesis 22.

apikoros—A heretic, one who is learned in Judaism but rejects it. The term evolved from the name of the Greek philosopher Epicurus.

Aramaic—A Semitic language, related to Hebrew and Arabic, which flourished in the Mesopotamian world in different forms from approximately 700 B.C.E. to the middle of the first millennium and is still spoken by small groups in Lebanon, Turkey, and Kurdistan. The language of the Talmud and other important Jewish texts, Aramaic was the lingua franca of the Jews in Greek and Roman times, and was used for rabbinic writings as late as the thirteenth century C.E.

Ashkenazi—Originally referred to Jews from Germany; eventually generalized to all Jews from Central and Eastern Europe.

ba'al teshuva—The Hebrew term for a Jew who has returned, i.e., become fully observant.

bar/bat mitzvah—A Jewish child becomes a bar or bat mitzvah, an adult member of the Jewish community who is able to fully participate in synagogue services and all other religious rituals, at the age of thirteen for boys and twelve for girls. The bar or bat mitzvah is usually celebrated by the youth being called to the Torah at synagogue services, followed by a party for friends and family.

blood libel—The anti-Jewish slander, first appearing in Norwich, England, in 1144, that Jews kill Christian children and use their blood for ritual purposes, especially on Passover. This slander occasionally still surfaces and has been the pretext for anti-Jewish violence over the centuries, leading to much death and destruction.

borscht belt—The string of Catskills summer resorts where Jews vacationed during much of the twentieth century.

bris—Short for bris milah, covenant of circumcision—the circumcision of eight-day-old Jewish boys as a sign of their entrance into the covenant of the Jewish people.

Chelm—A city in Poland, southeast of Lublin, which had a Jewish presence dating back perhaps as early as the twelfth century. Chelm appears often in Jewish folklore as a city populated by fools.

Chumash—From the Hebrew word for "five"; the Torah, also known as the Five Books of Moses or the Pentateuch, are often referred to as the Chumash.

diaspora—The Jewish communities outside the Land of Israel.

drash—A nonliteral commentary on a biblical verse.

"Eishet Chayil"— An excerpt of Proverbs 31, which a husband traditionally sings to his wife on Friday nights, enumerating her virtues.

Eretz Israel—The Land of Israel, historically a phrase employed by Zionists to refer to the Jewish presence in that location, which would eventually become the State of Israel.

Final Solution—The Nazi plan for the extermination of the Jewish people.

golden calf—The statue made by Aaron at the behest of the Israelites, who, uneasy about Moses' prolonged absence on Mount Sinai receiving the Ten Commandments, insisted that Aaron make a god for them.

Haggadah—The book that contains the text of the seder ritual performed on the first two nights of Passover.

Hashem—Literally, "the Name," used to refer to God when one does not want to use a more holy name of God.

Kabbalah—The Jewish mystical and esoteric traditions.

Kaddish—An Aramaic prayer praising God's eternal holiness. Several variations on the Kaddish are recited throughout synagogue services. Best known is the Mourner's Kaddish, recited by those who have lost a loved one. Kaddish prayers are said only when a minyan (a quorum of ten Jewish adults) is present.

kippah—The Hebrew term for the skullcap worn by Jews to show humility before God; a yarmulke.

Korah—The leader of the great rebellion against his cousins Moses and Aaron, in Numbers 16.

marranos—The hidden Jews of Christian Spain and Portugal who converted to Christianity but continued to live as Jews in secret. These New Christians were sought out and often killed by the Inquisition.

matzah—The unleavened bread eaten at Passover, in commemoration of the Israelites' hasty departure from Egypt, which occurred too quickly for the bread to rise. Also known as the bread of affliction, it symbolizes the suffering of the Jews in Egypt.

mezuzah—A parchment scroll on which are written several biblical passages, the mezuzah is placed inside a case and attached to the doorposts of rooms in Jewish homes in accordance with the biblical verses in Deuteronomy 6:9 and 11:20.

midrash—A method of exegesis of biblical texts; a legal, exegetical, or homelitical commentary on the Bible; see also *drash*.

mikvah—Ritual bath. In the time of the Temple in Jerusalem, the mikvah was used widely by priests and all those bringing sacrifices to the Temple. Since the Temple's destruction in the year 70 C.E., the mikvah continues to be used by women after their menstrual cycles, as well as for conversions, and by pious Jews on Sabbath and holiday eves.

mitzvot—Hebrew for commandments, referring to God's commandments.

Nineveh—The great city of Assyria to which God sends the prophet Jonah.

Ostjuden—The German term for Jews from Eastern Europe. German Jews, who were more assimilated into the surrounding culture in the late nineteenth and early twentieth centuries, often looked down on their eastern brethren as less cultured.

payot—The Hebrew word for the long earlocks worn by ultra-Orthodox Jewish men and boys. The Torah forbids taking a blade to shave the four corners of the face, which include the sideburns. While many observant Jewish men will trim their sideburns, the ultra-Orthodox let them grow long.

Pesach—The Passover holiday, commemorating the Exodus of the Israelites from Egypt, as well as celebrating the coming of spring.

pogrom—A state-sponsored anti-Jewish riot. Originally referred to anti-Jewish violence in Russia in the 1880s and 1890s; it now describes any violence against Jews.

Protocols of the Elders of Zion—An anti-Semitic forgery that purports to reveal the existence of a Jewish conspiracy for world domination. The notation of Jewish domination has its roots in anti-Semitic ideas that have existed since the Middle Ages but gained its greatest expression in the *Protocols*; first circulated in Russia in the 1890s, it has since been translated and disseminated worldwide.

Rav—Rabbi

responsa—The term for the continually evolving body of Jewish legal decisions developed as responses to questions posed to rabbis.

Rosh Hashanah—The Jewish New Year, the first of the Hebrew month of Tishrei, occurring in September or October. The holiday ushers in the ten days of repentance that culminate in Yom Kippur.

seder—From the Hebrew word for "order," the seder is the ritual meal on the first two nights of Passover at which the story of the Exodus is retold.

Shabbos—The Sabbath, the Jewish day of rest from Friday sundown to nightfall on Saturday.

shanda fun dem goyim—"A disgrace before the Gentiles." A Yiddish criticism of Jewish behavior of Jews that might embarrass coreligionists before the wider community.

Shema—An affirmation of faith in the one God, the Shema is one of the core prayers of the Jewish liturgy. It begins with Deuteronomy 6:4, Hear o Israel, the Lord Our God, the Lord is one, and continues through verse 9 and with passages from Deuteronomy 11 and Numbers 15.

Shoah—The Holocaust.

shteibl—A little synagogue, sometimes in someone's home.

shtetl—the Yiddish term for a small town or city, the term often connotes either a sense of parochialism or of nostalgia.

shul—Synagogue.

Shulkhan Arukh—Literally, "the set table," this law code completed in 1555 by Rabbi Joseph Caro, and amended shortly thereafter by Rabbi Moses Isserles, remains the authoritative code of law for observant Jews.

spies—In the book of Numbers, Moses sends twelve spies, one from each tribe, into the Land of Israel to see what challenges lie before them in conquering the land. Ten of the twelve spies report that the land is unconquerable, leading the Israelites to protest again their having left Egypt.

tallis—The shawl worn by adult Jews in prayer. The tallis is a four-cornered garment, with tassels tied on each corner, as per the commandment in Numbers 15 to tie fringes on the corners of the Jews' garments as a reminder of God's commandments.

Talmud—The Talmud, from the Hebrew word for "to learn," is the collected rabbinic teachings from the first through the fifth centuries. The Talmud comprises the Mishnah, the rabbinic teachings codified in the year 220 by Rabbi Judah the Prince, and the Gemara, the further rabbinic interpretations of the Mishnah, from the third through the fifth centuries. Rabbinic academies in Babylonia and in Israel each developed their own Talmud; the Babylonian is generally considered authoritative. The central text of Jewish Law, the Talmud is usually printed accompanied by later commentaries.

teshuva—Repentance.

Tevye—The main character of the musical *Fiddler on the Roof*, based on "Tevye the Dairyman" by the great Yiddish writer Sholem Aleichem.

Torah—The Five Books of Moses, comprising the first section of the Hebrew Bible. Also used more generally to refer to Jewish learning and Jewish texts.

trope—The musical cantillation used for the chanting of biblical texts.

Tu Bi'Shvat—The fifteenth day of the Hebrew month of Shvat (roughly corresponding to February), honored as the New Year of Trees.

yetzer hara—The evil impulse, the traditional Hebrew term for one's inclination to engage in bad behavior.

Yiddish—The primary spoken and written language of the Jews of Central and Eastern Europe during most of the last millennium. Written in Hebrew letters, the language probably developed around the eleventh century in German-speaking lands, fusing medieval German syntax and language with Hebrew and Aramaic terms. As Yiddish-speaking Jews migrated throughout Europe, local dialects developed that incorporated a wealth of words borrowed from Russian, French, Polish, and other languages.

yirat shamayim—Fear of Heaven, the proper awe-filled attitude in which a Jew should live his life.

Yom Kippur—The Day of Atonement. The holiest day of the Jewish year, it is the culmination of the ten days of repentance that begin on Rosh Hashanah. It is marked by abstinence from food, drink, bathing, and sexual activity, in order to spend the day in prayer, introspection, and repentance.

ABOUT THE AUTHOR

David Mamet is a Pulitzer Prize–winning playwright. He is the author of *Glengarry Glen Ross*, *The Cryptogram*, and *Boston Marriage*, among other plays. He has also published three novels and many screenplays, children's books, and essay collections. His work on Jewish subjects includes *The Old Religion*, a novel about the lynching of Leo Frank; *Bar Mitzvah* and *Passover*, two books for children; *Five Cities of Refuge*, a Torah commentary written with Rabbi Lawrence Kushner; and the film *Homicide*, which he wrote and directed.